Kristen Gilbert & Other Killer Nurses

Lynn Dilman

Published by Trellis Publishing, 2021.

KRISTEN GILBERT & OTHER KILLER NURSES

First edition. July 1, 2021.

ISBN: 979-8224708802

Written by Lynn Dilman.

KRISTEN GILBERT & OTHER KILLER NURSES

LYNN DILMAN

In the early 1990s, former Veterans Affairs (VA) nurse Kristen Gilbert was found guilty of murdering four of her patients – and convicted of attempting to murder two more. Gilbert is suspected to be responsible for the deaths of dozens more veterans who were under her care during her career as a nurse.

"Gilbert is a calculating predator," read an article in the October 8, 2000 edition of the Boston Globe, "nothing less than a serial murderer in a white lab coat who attacked her victims in at the Department of Veterans Affairs Medical Centre here with needles of poison. She struck, [prosecutors] say, as sick veterans lay in high-tech beds provided by their grateful government."

"Twisted, but not stupid."

Born to parents Richard and Claudia Strickland on November 13, 1967, Kristen Heather Strickland was the oldest of two daughters. The family seemed relatively happy, and both children seemed well adjusted. By the time Gilbert was a pre-teen, the Stricklands had relocated from Fall River to Groton, Massachusetts, and appeared to be a normal family.

According to the Boston Globe, Gilbert was, at that time, a typical teenager – she earned pocket money by babysitting the neighbourhood kids, she loved soap operas, she took the bus to school and found her honours classes to be a breeze. A star student, Gilbert even joined the math club, and her date to the 1985 graduation prom at Groton-Dunstable Regional High School was the smartest boy in her class.

"She was not hotheaded or anything like that," remembered John Moore, who had lived next door to the Strickland family in the picturesque New England village. "She was a great kid – a cute kid. She seemed decent and normal, pretty intelligent, sharp."

The Moore and Strickland families were tucked away in a private area off Boston Road, and the two families initially began socializing together. Gilbert's father, Richard, worked as an electronics executive, and Claudia was a part time teacher and a full time homemaker. The families even became relatively close, with Gilbert often taking care of the Moores' two kids when they all came home from school, until their parents returned home after work.

However, the two families eventually had a falling out – a spat Moore was unwilling to explain in detail to reporters. The relationship fell apart, and one day, the Moores looked out the window to see a moving van parked in front of the Strickland family's small two storey home.

"Next thing we knew – boom – they're gone," Moore added.

Although Gilbert's early childhood indicated no significant issues, things began to change as she grew older. Friends recall that Gilbert became a skilled liar, and regularly boasted that she was somehow related to Lizzie Borden, a serial killer from the 1800s who had been accused of brutally murdering her father and stepmother with an axe.

In addition to habitually lying, friends claimed, Gilbert was frequently manipulative. She also had a tendency to threaten to kill herself whenever she was upset, and according to court records, would occasionally even make more violent threats.

Investigators later heard from ex-boyfriends, who described Gilbert as a skilled manipulator, who was "twisted, but not stupid." According to their accounts, Gilbert was capable of some dangerous, attention seeking behaviour – histrionics that included things like tampering with their vehicles or clawing their skin with her fingernails.

One of Gilbert's high school boyfriends even recalled an incident where an upset Gilbert had left a fake suicide note where he would find it, in which she claimed that she'd eaten glass.

Even Gilbert's father spoke about his daughter's habitual lying with his own psychiatrist. While Richard Strickland assured the doctor it wasn't true, he recounted how in college, Gilbert had managed to convince her roommates that her mother Claudia was an alcoholic who became abusive when she drank.

"She lied a lot," admitted Alberta Erickson, who had resided in Groton just across the street from the Strickland family. Her own daughter had been a close friend of Gilbert's when the girls were younger. "She had this blank stare, as if she was trying to make things up as she went along. She was one strange girl."

Erickson even recalled Gilbert's attempts to establish a familial link between herself and Lizzie Borden – Gilbert would often brag about this "distant, unsubstantiated" connection.

According to Erickson's daughter, Pamela Smethurst, Gilbert's constant lying was what eventually ended their friendship. The two girls rode the school bus together, and spent enough time together for Smethurst to pick up on when Gilbert wasn't being truthful.

Smethurst still vividly remembers, after searching high and low for a favorite shirt, she saw Gilbert wearing it soon after. According to Gilbert, the shirt belonged to her – but Smethurst recognized the well loved article of clothing immediately.

"We used to sit and watch 'General Hospital,'" Smethurst said, noting that the soap opera had been on in the afternoons when the girls came home from school. "And – this sounds freaky and almost made up, now. But there was this one character in the show who was this evil nurse. And I remember [Gilbert] said, 'I like Amy.' And I said, 'Oh, my God! Why would you like Amy?' And she said, 'I just like Amy.'"

Amy was "conniving and backstabbing," Smethurst added, and said she remembered thinking, "This is kind of strange."

A "highly skillful" nurse

After graduating from high school, Gilbert pursued a degree as a registered nurse at Greenfield Community College, which she completed in 1988. She studied both microbiology and surgical nursing, but made little impression on her instructors during her schooling.

"We certainly don't graduate anyone we don't feel comfortable with taking care of you, or I, or any of our patients," said Jean A.

Simmons, the coordinator of the nursing program at Greenfield Community College.

She also married Glenn Gilbert that same year, at the age of 21. The couple had met at Hampton Beach, New Hampshire, and had wed after a courtship of just three years. Glenn worked for a local optical lens firm, and they bought a home together in 1989 – after Gilbert was hired by the Veterans Administration Medical Center in Northampton, Massachusetts.

Located in the Leeds section of Northampton, the hospital is tucked away on more than 100 acres of pine forested land, known in the community as Bear Hill. The area has an established history – originally, the site housed the old Solomon Warner Tavern, a watering stop for the 19th century Boston-Albany stagecoaches.

The land was cleared in 1922, and it became the location of the VA's very first psychiatric hospital just two years later. The current 191 bed facility sprawls across 26 colonial buildings, separated by more than six miles of twisting roads, fountains, and shady trees.

Gilbert started working at the facility on March 6, 1989. She was stationed in the main medical unit, housed in Building One. She was a good nurse, according to her fellow workers – competent and very dedicated to the position. Even more than that, Gilbert was the kind of co-worker who went above and beyond for the other staff at the hospital. She remembered everyone's birthday, and was always the one in charge of organizing the facility's annual gift exchange during the holidays.

"At Christmas time, [Gilbert] always made sure that we had like a secret Santa," said a VA nurse named Karin Abderhalden, who had worked with Gilbert at the hospital.

Together, Gilbert and Abderhalden set up gift drives to donate items to families in need, and Gilbert ran the hospital's "Sunshine Fund," which would provide bouquets of flowers to new parents, newlyweds, or colleagues who had fallen ill.

On the C Ward, where Gilbert was stationed, she was known as a social butterfly. But in addition to being both pretty and popular, Gilbert was a "highly skillful" nurse, according to her superiors – particularly when it came to emergency situations, where Gilbert's cool head and calm reactions made her a favorite among the doctors.

"She readily recognizes actual or potential changes in patients' conditions," read one of the proficiency reports filed about Gilbert. "She is highly skillful in medical emergencies. And she is calm and compassionate with the mentally compromised patient. She is routinely assigned to ICU."

And according to clinical nursing coordinator Bernard P. LaFlam, her supervisors at the VA "had no problems with her nursing skills."

Gilbert and her husband welcomed their first child to the family in late 1990 – a baby boy. When Gilbert returned from her medical leave, however, she didn't come back to work the same shift she'd worked previously. Instead, she switched to the 4 p.m. to midnight shift – and shortly after, odd things began taking place during the evening hours.

The medical center's death rate quickly grew to three times what it had been in the previous three years, because patients were constantly dying during Gilbert's shifts. But as each incident took place, Gilbert's competency as a nurse shone through, and the other evening shift staff admired her ability to handle herself in a crisis.

In 1993, Gilbert gave birth to a second child – but her marriage to Glenn Gilbert had already become fairly strained. She'd been spending an awful lot of time with a co-worker, James Perrault, who was a security guard at the medical facility. An Army veteran of the Persian Gulf War, Perrault had left a position as a security guard at a local department store to join the VA hospital's police force, which boasted eleven members.

"We enjoyed each other's company."
He started working at the hospital just six months after Gilbert switched to the evening shift. Although he was only making $5,000 a

year more than he'd earned hunting down shoplifters at the mall, the job at the VA was closer to what Perrault was ultimately hoping to achieve – legitimate police work.

While Perrault was on duty, VA policy dictated that he be required to respond to all cardiac emergencies, or "codes." When he wasn't dealing with codes or patrolling the roadways of the expansive hospital facility, however, Perrault was flirting with an attractive nurse who worked on Ward C – a nurse who seemed to always be involved whenever patients on the second floor medical unit of Building One faced cardiac arrest.

"During my rounds doing security, I stopped on the wards and I would talk to staff members," Perrault said. "And [Gilbert] and I seemed to have more in common, and we talked a lot."

When their shift ended at midnight, Gilbert would frequently go out socializing with Perrault and other hospital employees, instead of returning home to her husband and young children. They went to the VFW for beers – the Michael F. Curtain Post 8006 of the Veterans of Foreign Wars was only a mile away from the hospital's front doors.

Hidden away in the back of an old church, the large barroom offered $1.50 draft beers, a big screen TV, and a pool table. It was a great spot to unwind after work, and Perrault said Gilbert had hinted to him that her marriage had become increasingly rocky. When they emailed, Perrault said, she was seductive and funny, and soon, the conversations became sexually suggestive.

"After a few weeks of just flirting back and forth, we were down at the VFW, and after the VFW closed, I walked her out to her vehicle and we had a kiss," Perrault recalled.

By the end of the next year, Gilbert and Perrault had taken their relationship to the next level, and had begun a passionate extramarital affair. Gilbert's husband, Glenn, had met Perrault just once, on a summer boating excursion. But for some reason, as Gilbert's affair grew more serious, she started spending more time preparing home cooked meals for her husband.

And then, he noticed that his suppers didn't taste right.

"He told one witness that it was her goal to have her husband out of the house by Thanksgiving," prosecutors explained during a pretrial motion.

According to the prosecution, Gilbert had started lacing her husband's food with trace amounts of diuretics – a drug that would have been easy for her to obtain at work. Diuretics help to increase the body's discharge of urine, but Glenn Gilbert became violently ill on the evening of November 5, 1995.

After Gilbert drove her sick husband to the emergency room and he was examined by doctors, it was confirmed that he was suffering from low potassium and glucose levels. He was treated at the facility and then sent home.

But he got sick again just a week later. While Gilbert argues the incident was simply a harmless fainting spell as she'd been attempting to care for her husband, prosecutors claim it was an attempted murder.

Glenn's account of that day began when his wife had come home on her dinner break that evening. She told Glenn that she wasn't satisfied with the care he'd received at the local civilian hospital they'd visited, and that she wanted to draw a blood sample on her own to have it tested at the VA hospital, instead.

In the bathroom, Gilbert took two syringes from a canvas bag she'd brought home with her. In one of the syringes, Glenn saw a clear, odorless liquid – Gilbert assured him it was just a saline solution. She told him she was going to use it to flush his vein before she started drawing blood, a non-standard procedure which can potentially be dangerous.

She wrapped a tourniquet around his arm and inserted the needle. According to Glenn's account, "once the needle went in, his arm grew cold." The color began to drain from his chest and down his arms, and he said he attempted to pull himself away from his wife and asked her to please take the needle out. Instead, however, prosecutors said Glenn's testimony would be that Gilbert then "pinned him against the wall with her hip" and proceeded with the injection.

Then, Glenn said, he felt himself losing consciousness and slid down the wall to the bathroom floor.

Moments later, however, he awoke to see his wife – appearing flustered – shoving the syringes back into the canvas bag. He said Gilbert told him he'd just fainted at the sight of the needle, and added, "this was not going to work."

To Glenn, the incident was insignificant enough that he never even thought to tell the police. It was only brought up months later, during a custody dispute after Gilbert had made the decision to leave her family. But according to the authorities, the incident seemed to indicate that Gilbert may have been considering the possibility of murdering her husband.

"If it were the defendant's intent to kill her husband, one would have to wonder why she did not complete the act after he had slumped helplessly to the floor," Gilbert's defense team argued in a court brief.

While Glenn struggled to understand what had happened on the bathroom floor, and what his wife might be doing to his meals, Gilbert and Perrault were considering their options for the next step in their affair.

Although she'd offered up no proof, Gilbert had told Perrault that her husband had become abusive – and Perrault had reached the end of his rope.

"We had been at the Holyoke Mall, having breakfast, and during breakfast, I explained to her that because her husband had been abusing her, as she alleged, that if she did not leave him, I would leave her," Perrault admitted.

Immediately, he said, Gilbert burst into tears, but then walked over to the nearest pay phone and placed a call to Glenn. Perrault said he was close enough to hear Gilbert tell him that she was leaving him.

Glenn said he was trying to do what he could "to save the marriage, at that time." However, he wasn't a fan of his wife's new friend – "I disliked [Perrault's] character."

Within a week, Gilbert had moved out of the family's home, leaving the kids to live with their father. She found a small apartment in Easthampton, just a few blocks away from where Perrault lived. He helped her settle into her new apartment, and she rewarded him with his own key.

"We enjoyed each other's company," Perrault confessed.

From shift to shift

Gilbert continued to work at the hospital – but the deaths that seemed to occur all too often during Gilbert's shifts had aroused the suspicions of her co-workers. According to Frank Bertrand, a VA nurse who had resuscitated one of the elderly patients Gilbert had allegedly tried to kill, it almost seemed like she was two people at once.

"Things with [Gilbert] weren't always the way they seemed," he said. "I don't know if she had two personalities or something that she could turn on or turn off, much like an actor playing a role."

According to assistant US attorney William M. Welch II, when Gilbert started working the evening shift in the later part of 1991, the death rate on that shift tripled – while the death rate on the overnight shift, which she had stopped working in 1990, dropped back to the level it had been in 1988, before Gilbert accepted the $40,000 a year position with the VA.

"So, in essence, deaths followed Gilbert as she switched from shift to shift to shift," said Welch during a hearing ahead of Gilbert's trial.

But Gilbert's lawyer, Harry L. Miles, said the statistics indicating the rise in the hospital's mortality rate were "misleading."

"The problem with [that] evidence is that it tells you that an extremely skillful, extremely conscientious nurse can be singled out as having killed people because she acted conscientiously and competently," he argued at a hearing.

While many of the patients who passed away were elderly or already experiencing failing health, others were somewhat difficult to explain. Despite having no prior history of heart problems, patients were dying of cardiac arrest.

And, hospital workers had noticed, they always seemed to be low on ephedrine – a drug that, administered incorrectly, had the potential to cause heart failure.

Over the span of a few months, in late 1995 and early 1996, four of Gilbert's patients died. The cause of death was listed as cardiac arrest – and in each of the four cases, the suspected reason for the heart failure was an overdose of ephedrine. Once several of Gilbert's co-workers raised concerns about her possible involvement in the deaths, an investigation was launched at the hospital.

Gilbert resigned from her position shortly after, claiming she'd sustained injuries while on the job and needed time off to recover.

The relationship between Gilbert and Perrault also began to crumble, in the summer of 1996. That September, during the federal investigation into the high death rate at the VA hospital, authorities brought Perrault in for questioning.

And then, the bomb threats started.

While working at the hospital on September 26, Perrault answered a call from someone who claimed that they'd planted three bombs within the facility. The police were called down to the hospital, and patients were carefully evacuated from the building, but a search of the facility revealed that no explosives had been hidden inside.

A similar threat was made the following day, and again on September 30th – all while Perrault was working. It didn't take long for police to link Gilbert to the series of calls. In January of 1998, she was tried and convicted of making bomb threats, and received a sentence of 15 months in prison.

Federal investigators, though, weren't satisfied. They were compiling evidence to build a case against Gilbert, for her involvement with the increased cardiac deaths at the VA facility. By November of that year, Gilbert faced a new trial – for the killing of Henry Hudon, Kenneth Cutting, and Edward Skwira.

She was also charged with attempted murder in two other cases, the deaths of Thomas Callahan and Angelo Vella, and by May of 1999, she'd been charged again, in the death of a patient named Stanley Jagodowski.

"Just after leaving, one of the nurses saw Gilbert go into Jagodowski's room with a needle and a swab in her hand, under the pretext of 'flushing' his intravenous line with 'saline' to keep the line open," read court papers by Assistant US Attorneys William M. Welch II and Ariane D. Vuono.

However, Jagodowski hadn't been prescribed any injections – all of his medications were administered orally.

"[Gilbert] and Jagodowski were in the room alone when the [other] nurse heard Jagodowski yell, 'Ow, it hurts! You're killing me!'" prosecutors claimed. "As the nurse turned towards Jagodowski's room, she observed [Gilbert] exit."

Just a few minutes later, Jagodowski had suffered cardiac arrest – and within the next three hours, he would be dead. According to prosectors, his death was caused by Gilbert, who had used a heart stimulant – epinephrine – to push him into heart failure.

Doing it for the attention

During the November 2000 trial, prosecutors theorized that Gilbert had committed the murders in an attempt to spend more time with Perrault – she craved attention, they said. Of the 350 recorded patient deaths over the seven years Gilbert spent working at the hospital, she was on duty for more than half of them.

"The chance of that being a coincidence, [prosecutors] calculate, is 1 in 100 million," stated a Boston Globe article from October 8, 2000.

Prosecutors allege that Gilbert injected her patients with synthetic adrenaline, which "converted their hearts into fatally revved up and out of control pumps," according to the Boston Globe. It was an opportunity for Gilbert to show off for Perrault, they claimed.

"She liked the attention it brought," said Welch.

Welch added the prosecution intended to seek the death penalty, if the jury found Gilbert guilty of capital murder. The prospect "horrifies" the former nurse, according to the Boston Globe. Having already endured two and a half years in jail by the time the case went to trial, Gilbert was a shadow of her past self – her "fashionable blonde hair," attractive appearance, and glowing complexion had withered away, leaving her pallid, overweight, and mousy haired.

Still, she claims, she's no killer. Defense lawyers continued to argue that the patients had all died of natural causes, and claimed Gilbert was completely innocent.

"It's an unimaginable strain to be on trial for first degree murder, let alone looking at the death penalty," said David P. Hoose, Gilbert's defense attorney. "She has been absolutely adamant that she has done nothing wrong to any patient at the VA."

Her patients were all old, Gilbert argued. They had weak hearts, and were already sick. Some of them had even been diagnosed with terminal diseases. Her needles were used, according to Gilbert, to "comfort and heal." Not to inflict pain or damage.

"All of the people who died, died of natural causes. It's up to [the prosecution] to prove, beyond a reasonable doubt, some unnatural cause," said Gilbert's other court-appointed attorney, Harry L. Miles. "And we're saying they can't do it. There's certainly no eye witness saying that they saw her inject anybody with a substance. And there's no outright confession."

Even her co-workers had a difficult time accepting the idea that someone they had spent so many hours with could be capable of something so evil.

"Imagine having to testify against somebody who you worked closely with for a number of years on a matter like this – someone you liked and got to know and got to know their husband and their kids," said nurse Bertrand. "It bothers some people quite a bit. Who would ever suspect something like this?"

Jurors returned with a verdict on March 14, 2001. In three of the four cases, the jury determined Gilbert was guilty of first degree murder, and in the fourth, she was found guilty of second degree murder. She also received convictions for the attempted murders of the two other patients, and was sentenced to four consecutive terms of life in prison.

While Gilbert had initially attempted to appeal the sentence, she dropped the application in 2003. She remains behind bars in a federal prison in Texas.

KIMBERLY SAENZ

JAMIE PARKS

Kimberly Clark Saenz was a nurse. Almost ten years ago now, in 2008, she worked in a clinic called the DaVita Lufkin Dialysis Center. The clinic was- and still is- in Lufkin, a small blue collar city in East Texas of around 33,000 souls. But rather than care for her patients, she decided to kill. Because of a home life fraught with difficulties- she and her husband has fought, he had filed for divorce, and even taken out a restraining order against her- Kimberly's unrestrained and misdirected anger was taken out on her patients. And this was just the latest in a long list of healthcare jobs that Kimberly had held, after a spate of firings for various misdemeanours.

Even though she worked in a dialysis center, where there is normally little to cause complications and death, the number of patients dying on her watch alerted and disturbed other hospital staff. Even so, it took far too long for her managers and the authorities to find out what she had been doing. When, to their horror, they uncovered her crimes, Kimberly became national news.

Who was Kimberly Clark Saenz?

Kimberly hadn't had the best start in life. She was born Kimberly Clark Fowler in Fall River, Massachusetts in 1973. After an uneventful childhood during which she moved away from Massachusetts to Texas, she dropped out of high school in her senior year after falling pregnant. Kimberly and her husband would go on to have two children together, but Kimberly struggled with addiction and the strains this put on her home life.

She suffered from substance abuse problems, which proved to be a drain on the family finances; it was also enough to convince her to steal, which she did time and time again from her various employers. According to witness testimony at her trial, Lufkin law enforcement told the court that she had been arrested multiple times for intoxication and criminal trespass after domestic disturbances with her husband, Kevin Mark Saenz. She was clearly unhappy with the direction in which her life was heading.

Before taking the nursing position that would prove to be her last, Kimberly had been fired from four similar jobs in the recent past. Each time had been because she was caught stealing medication in her handbag once her shift was over. What is worse is that she lied each time to her prospective employer, claiming that she had no criminal history to speak of, even though when she applied for her final care work position she had actually been on bail. In this way it would be fair to say that the deaths Kimberly caused were as much as anything because of a failure of oversight, and a failure to correctly check employees' criminal histories.

But in the end, it took a letter from a top fire official to actually get the matter investigated. The letter was sent anonymously, but complained of the highly unusual number of patients being transferred to hospital. The letter was sent in April 2008, and read 'In the last two weeks, we have transported 16 patients. This seems a little abnormal and disturbing to my med crews. Could these calls be investigated by you?'

Surveyors arrived within the next few days to try and get a handle on the situation. But if anything, this blew the case wide open: they realised that over the course of the preceding month, emergency crews had been called out a total of thirty times, seven of whom had cardiac problems, and four of whom died. To anybody unaware of the normal operation of a dialysis center, this may or may not have seemed excessive; but in comparison to the previous fifteen months before then, emergency services had only been required *twice,* according to the Texas Department of Health Services. Because of the strict quality controls involved in green lighting medical equipment and medicine for public use, all signs pointed to another cause: a person.

How was Kimberly caught?

Kimberly was eventually caught out because of her own brazen attitude to the crimes she committed. More of the details would come out once the case was brought to trial, but a number of eye witnesses had separately and independently told Kimberly's superiors that they had seen her poisoning the people she was supposed to care for. On the morning of April 28th, Kimberly arrived at work at 4:30am, only to be told that she was no longer on the rota to work as patient care technician- in charge of medication- she was to work as a simple patient monitor, who would check up on patients over the course of the day, and perform basic cleaning duties. According to her supervisor Amy Clinton, Kimberly's response was strange: she began crying, wiping away tears, and said that that particular job was beneath her. Amy had only been working at the DaVita clinic for a few days, and had been called in because of two recent and unusual deaths.

At 6am, the two witnesses were brought to the clinic- Lurlene Hamilton and Linda Hall. They were suffering with failing kidneys, and dialysis was not unusual for either of them; indeed, patients often undergo the treatment at least three times a week, and the procedure can take hours. There's little to do but sit, read, or talk to family or other patients. They were around 40 feet away from another two patients named Marva Rhone and Carolyn Risinger. They watched as Kimberly Saenz poured bleach from a jug into a cleaning bucket, and then as she drew up a small amount of the bleach into a syringe. This first concerned the witnesses because they felt that whatever the bleach was being used for, the bucket was most likely an unsanitary place to draw it from.

But what shocked them was what happened next. Kimberly approached the two patients, Rhone and Risinger, and injected the bleach into the feed lines of the dialysis machines that they were hooked up to. Fortunately, neither went into cardiac arrest, presumably because Kimberly did not or could not inject enough bleach into the system. But the eyewitness testimony of Hamilton and Hall was proven correct during later analysis, which found bleach in Rhone's dialysis line. Bleach, of course, has a terrible effect on the body; it easily eats through tissue and when injected into the blood can cause blood cells to burst. Because of the overload of potassium this can cause in the blood stream, cardiac arrest often immediately ensues. That being said, bleach is generally eliminated from the body quite quickly, and if the victim survives, they very rarely suffer any further lasting effects.

A key point to understand is that bleach is regularly used in dialysis clinics across the country. First, of course, for general cleaning of the floors and walls: blood is easily spilled and contamination is a major risk. But in addition, bleach is the most common cleaning fluid used to clear dialysis lines after being used. As such, there are strict guidelines over its use: it should be clear that injecting it into the dialysis lines while still in use by patients is against those guidelines!

In addition to this eyewitness testimony, after just a brief analysis of the rota, one of the inspectors found that Kimberly had been working on a staggering 84% of the shifts when a patient suffered either chest pain or cardiac arrest. She had been working there in an entry level position for eight months up until that point, and this bizarre discrepancy was enough to get Kimberly fired in April 2008.

On the same night as those final attacks, Lufkin Police officer of thirteen years Bradley Baker was called out to Mark Kevin Saenz's home at around 8:30pm. The couple had split not long ago. Baker described what happened next during his testimony at trial: "Ms. Saenz was banging on the door of the house. Her eyes were glassy and she was having trouble answering questions." Baker issued a criminal trespass warrant to Kimberly, and upon talking to her further she admitted that she was taking Cymbalta and drinking. She was arrested for public intoxication, and at this point, the police knew nothing of what she had done earlier that day at the dialysis clinic.

Kimberly on trial

When Kimberly was brought to trial, she faced five separate murder charges over the deaths of Clara Strange, Thelma Metcalf, Garlin Kelley, Cora Bryant and Opal Few. She was accused of having killed them through poisoning them with sodium hypochlorite- better known to us as bleach- through injecting it into their dialysis lines. In fact, two eyewitnesses claimed that she had attacked two different patients on the date of April 28th, 2008. Her attorneys argued that she had been set up: she was a scapegoat for the DaVita clinic, which had been failing its patients long before the spate of deaths that April in 2008.

The two witnesses, Linda Hall and Leraline Hamilton, claimed that those two patients- Marva Rhone and Carolyn Risinger- had been injected with bleach that day. In addition, the Food and Drug Administration (FDA) prepared a report which confirmed that samples from a number of the victims had indeed tested positive for bleach, and while other samples were unclear, there was evidence that bleach "may have been present at one time." To come to that conclusion, they examined blood tubing, syringes and IV bags which had been used for the patients' dialysis.

The information about Saenz that came out during trial was shocking, and did nothing to dispel the idea that she should never have been allowed in a position of care. She had previously been fired from Woodland Heights hospital for stealing Demerol, which had been found in her handbag at the end of a shift. Very soon after having been fired from the DaVita clinic, she was suspended from the profession and her nursing licence was taken away. In between her firing and the trial, she worked as a receptionist without disclosing why she had been forced to find employment.

Kimberly refused to take the stand in her own defence, but her lawyers argued that she was a good woman who could never fathom killing another human being. 'Kimberly Saenz is a good nurse, a compassionate, a caring individual who assisted her patients and was well liked,' one of her defense attorneys, T. Ryan Deaton, told the court. And in a pre-recorded video message, Kimberly told the court that she felt 'railroaded' by the clinic; she had been the fall guy for the clinic, which desperately needed somebody to pin their failings on.

Her defense team argued that the marital issues and family strife she had been through prior to the murders had been overemphasised by the prosecution. To try and prove their point, they called upon an extensive number of character witnesses who each testified that Kimberly was not the woman she was made out to be in the press. If anything, she was a good woman, a caring woman who loved her family despite her struggles with addiction.

The first witness they called upon was Vernon Dean Warren, who had been dating Mark Saenz's mother at the time of the murders. He testified that he held no ill will against her at all, and that she was welcome to his home anytime. A friend of Kim's, Peggy Wells, also took to the stand to defend her friend. She had met Saenz in kindergarten, so had known her for well over thirty years. Peggy felt that Kimberly was no danger to either society or to her children.

Next up for the defence was Wendy Bryan, who had met Kimberly while she worked at Fleetwood Transportation, and where Kimberly had worked for several years. She told the packed courtroom that Kimberly had been a model employee, and that her personal troubles should not cloud anybody's mind about the person Kimberly really was. Asked about whether she felt that Kimberly was a good employee and a good person despite her personal issues, Wendy responded: "I would have absolutely hired her. Absolutely, without a doubt."

Another former employee of Fleetwood Transportation, Tonya Monlar, testified that Kimberly was "a very hard worker, very thorough." She even said that no matter what the outcome of the trial turned out to be, she would still keep in touch with Kimberly because she believed her to be a genuine and good person. "If I can visit, I'll visit. I'll write, and she's always in my prayers," she told the court. Yet another character witness was Barbara Allen, who had taught both Kim Saenz and her son. She told the court that Kimberly was a caring mother who had sacrificed her own schooling to go through with having her firstborn despite being so young. The local elementary school principal described how Kim was dedicated to her son: "When [he] was younger, he played baseball with my son. Kim was always there," said Karen Schumaker. And she described Kim's daughter as "a great kid".

Kimberly had sworn in an affidavit that she had no criminal record whatsoever, but a basic check revealed her extensive list of felonies: including the overuse and misuse of prescription drugs, general substance abuse problems, theft and violence. Prosecutors branded her defence a joke, calling it 'absolutely ridiculous'. They painted her as both a depressed and disgruntled employee, who on the testimony of her fellow nurses was always complaining about her patients, in particular those who required extensive care. They had even found evidence from her computer that she had searched for information on the Internet about bleach poisoning, whether bleach could poison a person through being injected into the blood, and whether bleach was traceable.

At one point in the trial, the victims of Kimberly's crimes were encouraged to speak and testify as to the misery she had caused. Thelma Metcalf's daughter told Kimberly: "You are nothing more than a psychopathic serial killer. I hope you burn in hell". The prosecution were also completely straightforward in their assessment of Kimberly's role and her obvious guilt: "The only days there were deaths in April, she was there," the attorney for the prosecution said. "Dialysis patients are sick, but every source of information we can find says it is very unusual for patients to die during dialysis treatment."

The attorney for the prosecution was Clyde Herrington. He believed that there were far more victims than those which were being discussed at the trial, an opinion based on the research of an epidemiologist at the Center for Disease Control and Prevention. That research categorically connected Saenz to the crimes, so it was a shame that Lufkin Police detectives were only able to find evidence from the two weeks prior to Kimberly being sacked. As such, there was nowhere near enough evidence to bring a successful case for those other victims; although given Kimberly's obvious guilt, and her modus operandi, it was plain to see that she had done far more damage than the few victims she was on trial for.

Kimberly's defense knew that she stood little chance of being found innocent of the charge of murder. So, rather than argue for her to be set free, they tried to have her charge of capital murder reduced to one of first degree murder- in other words, she would be in prison for life no matter what, but could avoid the death penalty. In summary, another of Kimberly's defense attorneys named Steve Taylor told the jury "She's never getting out no matter what you do... Society is protected. You will never see her again." Taylor also pointed out to the jury that Kimberly had been free during the period of the trial, and that prosecutors could not demonstrate that she had been a danger to the public.

To prove their point, the defense brought in Frank G. AuBuchon, a retired former employee of the Texas Department of Criminal Justice. Through him, the defense wanted to prove that just because they were pushing for something other than the death sentence, that Kimberly could never be a danger to the community again. Describing Kimberly's probable sentence, AuBuchon said: "It's a true life sentence. These people will die in custody." On the topic of what her life behind bars would be like, he said "You very quickly in prison the easiest way to do your time is to behave yourself. You get more privileges... Mind your own business. Don't tell anybody why you're there. Obey the rules." Finally, Frank Taylor told the court: "You will never see them again in society. They belong in another society now, the prison society."

On the other hand, during their summation, the prosecution did not specifically push for the death penalty. But they did remind the jury of Kimberly's criminal past, her issues with prescription drugs, and her propensity to lie to get what she wants. Just before the jurors retired to consider their verdict, Clyde Herrington told them: "I know you'll reach a verdict that's just and in accordance with the law," while showing them photos of the many victims who had suffered and died because of Kimberly and her actions. It was the prosecution that got what they wanted.

Kimberly was found guilty on March 31st, 2012, on the charge of capital murder, which covered each of the five murders. It was also clear that she had attacked, injured and killed far more patients than just those five. Just a few days afterwards, on April 2nd 2012, the jury sentenced Kimberly on behalf of Angelina County to life in prison with no hope of parole, and three separate twenty year sentences for aggravated assault. She remains in prison to this day.

What made Kimberly kill?

For anybody with even a passing knowledge of true crime, 'nurses who kill' are a recognisable and uniquely interesting subgroup of serial killers who continue to fascinate the American public. Genene Jones killed anywhere between six and sixty infants as a pediatric nurse in the '70s; Kristen Gilbert, 'the Angel of Death' killed four and tried to kill two more with epinephrine as a nurse in Massachusetts. Judy Buenoano, another nurse, was sentenced to die by electric chair for killing a string of previous husbands.

This isn't to suggest that there's something horrible about nurses! But the same trope is seen across the globe. Take Britain's Harold Shipman for instance: one of the UK's most infamous serial killers was a doctor, not a nurse, but killed at least 250 people over the course of decades. Each of these cases is tied to the others by the unique horror of killers who were supposed to care; murderers who were supposed to cure.

They are also linked by the fact that the underlying cause of all this misery and death is often inexplicable. Harold Shipman, for example, never expressed guilt or remorse. He maintained his innocence until his suicide in prison, as did his wife Primrose. As part of their case against Kimberly, the prosecution didn't actually have to prove her motive. But Clyde Herrington did speak to a registered nurse, one who had done extensive research into nurses and doctors who kill. But her research-which took in over a hundred killers- couldn't point to any unifying motive.

As Herrington put it to the jury, "Criminal behavior is something we've been trying to understand since Cain killed Abel. Only when the health care killer confesses do we know motive." But what Herrington claimed was that Kimberly had been driven to kill by her own troubles with both prescription drugs and her failing marriage. "From talking to some of the folks who worked with her, it sounded like her husband didn't want her to quit (DaVita)," Herrington continued. "She was depressed. She was frustrated, and I think she took those frustrations out on the patients."

How did Kimberly get away with her crimes for so long?

Kimberly Saenz's defense attorney, Ryan Deaton, claimed that the DaVita clinic was already plagued by malpractice and unusual deaths long before Kimberly started working there. Prior to the beginning of the trial, Deaton had fought hard for the jury to be able to see a report by the U.S. Department of Health and Human Services, which had been heavily critical of the DaVita clinic and its working practices. It had been ruled inadmissible by the state District Judge, Barry Bryan.

The report supposedly claimed that from December 1st 2007 until April 28th 2008, the clinic had overseen nineteen deaths, while over the entirety of 2007 there had been 25. Overall, this put the clinic above the state average, but only by seven percent.

But more importantly, the DaVita clinic was also accused within this report of shoddy record keeping that put patients at risk. Over the period between September 1st 2007 and April 26th 2008, 102 patients from the DaVita clinic had been transported to a local hospital either during or immediately after their dialysis treatment. Of these 102 patients, 68 cases had not been fully written up with a complete adverse occurrence report. So even though it was undoubtedly Kimberly who killed those people- there was no other way for bleach to make its way into the dialysis machines, and she was seen by two separate eyewitnesses with the syringe filled with bleach in her hand- the shoddy record keeping allowed an environment in which somebody who wanted to do what Kimberly did could get away with it.

The report summarised its findings with a damaging conclusion on the DaVita clinic and the ability of its staff. Their findings suggested that the DaVita clinic and its staff "did not demonstrate competence in monitoring patients during treatment alerting nurses or physicians of changes to a patient's condition and following the physician's orders for the dialysis treatment." In response a spokesman for the DaVita clinic, Vince Hancock, said that the company's actions did not lead to any deaths in April 2008, and that the court case proved it. "We hope that healing can start to occur for families of victims and for our teammates who also have been victimized by the murderous acts of Kim Saenz," he told the press.

Kimberly's retrial

Unbelievably, Kimberly and her defense lawyers felt that she stood a chance of winning an appeal, and they immediately sought leave to fight their case in the Court of Appeals. But the judgment of her first trial was upheld in a decision issued in August 2015. "Although both the jury charge and argument of counsel weigh in favor of egregious harm, we conclude the state of the evidence and the record as a whole substantially support a finding of guilt in regard to each of the capital murder victims," the opinion stated. "Accordingly, we hold the record does not establish egregious harm, and we affirm the trial courts judgment."

One of the central points of the appeal was that the Angelina County district court had allowed the jury to find her guilty, even though they could not unanimously agree on which exact patients had been killed by Kimberly; the judge had felt it to be obvious enough that she had killed at least some of the patients who had died, due to circumstantial evidence and eyewitness accounts.

The court dismissed each of the 21 issues which Saenz put before them, and had initially issued their ruling on January 22nd, 2014, but this ruling was itself overruled in December of that same year by the Texas Court of Criminal Appeals. The appeal was then sent *back* to the Fourth Court of Appeals, but she was again unsuccessful. Herrington, the original attorney for the prosecution, claimed that she would have appealed no matter what the grounds, but he didn't think she would be very successful. "Kim Saenz is sentenced to a life without parole," Herrington said. "She has absolutely no reason to continue to appeal as long as the possibility even exists."

Kimberly remains in prison to this day, universally considered guilty of the crimes she was sentenced to. She has no chance of parole; the only downside is that we may never know exactly what motivated her to kill.

KILLER NURSE BEVERLY ALLITT

JENNIFER PARRIS

Beverly Allitt-the Angel of Death

It is hard to believe that a young female could be capable of murder, let alone multiple murders. It is even more shocking that a female nurse could carry out such terrible crimes. That is exactly what Beverly Allitt did though. This nurse is Britain's most infamous female serial killer and also goes by the name of the Angel of Death due to her responsibility to care for others but instead used her nursing position to kill people. Over a short period of fifty-nine days in her job as a nurse in a children's ward, she killed four young children and attempted to kill at least nine others either by causing cardiac arrest or hypoglycemia. The Angel of Death did not appear to be an evil killer though. She was very well mannered with parents, which is how she gained their trust with their precious loved ones. But after similar/suspicious causes of death in the children's ward, investigations at the hospital showed missing nursing records and the presence of Allitt with every one of those cases.

Childhood

As a child, Beverly Allitt liked attention and would go about negative ways of getting it. She was born in October of 1968 and was one of four children (two sisters and one brother). Her father worked in an off-licence (a British shop where the liquor is sold off premises) and her mother cleaned schools. Neighbors described Allitt as affectionate because she liked to volunteer and often would babysit. She did her chores at home and saved the money she earned. Teachers also really liked her and was considered one of their favorites. She went to school at Charles Read Secondary Modern School because she failed the exam needed to attend Kesteven and Grantham Girls' School.

She often would wear casts and bandages as a kid without letting her injuries be examined. She got worse as she got older and became overweight. During this time in her life, she was sick and injured more frequently. She often engaged in self-injury and spent a lot of time in and out of various hospitals due to different ailments such as gall bladder pain, back trouble, ulcers, headaches, and blurred vision, just to name a few. Her reasons were that she had been hit on her bike by a passing car or had fallen off a horse or even had been burned. Most of her problems were either made up or self-inflicted. She convinced a doctor to take out her healthy appendix. Then, she constantly interfered with the scar to keep it from healing. Another time, she stabbed herself in the hospital with the intention of injecting her body with water. Next, there was the time when she tampered with a thermometer in the hospital. Because she was physically healthy, she had to see lots of different doctors in order to keep them treating her.

Allitt was a frequent liar and not just about her illnesses. She would often make up stories. One time, she told people that her parents had split up and that she would have to go live with her aunt. The tales would be investigated and found out to not be true.

Beverly Allitt dreamed of becoming a nurse and attended school at Grantham College and began her studies at the age of sixteen. During her last year of school, she was absent approximately one hundred and twenty-six days with numerous illnesses. Nurses there also described her as odd. There were some at the school that thought Allitt would benefit from psychiatric help.

She did manage to find a boyfriend at Grantham College really only because she forced Stephen Biggs to be hers. He bought her a ring but she never set a date for the wedding and refused to hold his hand in public. Once, she faked a pregnancy. She said that Stephen had AIDS. Another time, she lied about being raped by a former boyfriend. Allitt was described as deceptive by her boyfriend.

Eventually, Allitt's odd injuries (real or fake) were thought to be from a controversial personality disorder known as Munchausen Syndrome. People with this disorder like to be ill because of the attention they get from others when they are sick as well as the satisfaction of fooling doctors with their self-inflicted illnesses and injuries. They often have long medical histories. They are frequent liars and have lab tests that lead to no answers for the doctors to diagnose a patient. Allitt may have liked the attention because even though her childhood seemed to be relatively normal, there could have been emotional needs that were not being met.

Nursing Career

Beverly Allitt went on to become a nurse but the odd behavior from her childhood still continued. She took her nursing exams and actually failed them because she was absent quite often due to her various illnesses.

After that, Allitt managed to find a job at a nursing home. Like at school, she was gone quite often. Once, when she was there, it was thought that she smeared feces on the walls.

In 1991, at the age of twenty-three, Beverly Allitt surprisingly got a six-month contract job at Grantham and Kesteven Hospital that is located in Lincolnshire working in the children's ward. This ward was for newborn babies up to the age of sixteen. Kids sent to this hospital often had minor illnesses. They were quickly treated and then sent home as soon as they were well.

When Allitt arrived at the hospital, she had had less than two years of experience at this point and was not even a qualified children's nurse. It was shocking that she even was considered for a job considering how many days of class she missed when attending nursing school. The only reason she got the job was because the hospital was understaffed and no one else applied for the job. At the time, there were only two day nurses and one night nurse. According to one of those nurses, Mary Reet, who worked at the hospital at the same time as Allitt, "There was something about her that I didn't like but couldn't pinpoint it" (Birmingham Mail). She thought that she seemed cheerful, friendly, and helpful, however. Allitt was even respected. She was the one calling the alarms and identifying problems that the very sick children were experiencing.

Because of her job working with others, it meant that she was no longer getting personal attention but it allowed her to find attention in other ways that were just as negative as when she was a kid. The nurse was able to use this opportunity to get close to the patients. Allitt was able to befriend all of her patients' parents by suggesting that they leave to go get some coffee. Through this recommendation, the parents were trusting her and allowing her to be alone to administer treatment to the children. The parents had really appreciated the nurse at the time because of her actions during this difficult time when their children were sick. It was her care and love for her patients that caused the parents to call her an angel. She would even ride with the patients in the ambulance if they needed to be transferred to another hospital. However, Allitt was far from an angel. The term *Angel of Death* is given to medical professionals that are supposed to be healing patients but are really causing them harm.

The angel changed a week after she arrived at the hospital and odd things began to happen. Money was being stolen from the nurses. A key to the insulin refrigerator had disappeared. This is also when the young patients began experiencing odd symptoms that were very serious. Some of the patients died. At Grantham and Kesteven Hospital, usually only one child died a year. Once Allitt started working, four children died in just a period of a few months.

The Victims

Allitt's reign of terror began on February 21, 1991. Though it is not exactly clear how many children she actually did harm, the definite numbers are four murders and nine that were purposely harmed all within a fifty-nine-day time period. The ages of her patients were between seventeen weeks to eleven years old.

Seven-month-old Liam Taylor was Beverly Allitt's first victim. He had a chest infection and had come to the hospital for treatment. Since Allitt was able to befriend the parents, they left the hospital to get some rest. Once they returned, they learned from her that Liam had experienced respiratory problems but had recovered. She tried to convince the parents to leave again but they chose to stay. He suffered more respiratory problems under Allitt. She let the emergency team at the hospital know once he started becoming pale. The other nurses on the floor were confused because no alarms sounded when he had stopped breathing. He did survive but he had suffered cardiac arrest and brain damage. He was put on life support and was later taken off of it by his parents. His death at the time was ruled as heart failure.

Timothy Hardwick was Allitt's next victim. He was the oldest victim at eleven. He had cerebral palsy and dealt with seizures. The emergency team was notified when the boy turned blue and had no pulse. Allitt stood by as the defibrillator was used. Unfortunately, the boy died. There was an autopsy performed but there were no answers to the cause of his death. Epilepsy was eventually ruled as the cause.

The third victim was one-year-old Kayley Desmond. She had a chest infection but was getting better. After being in the care of Allitt though, she went into cardiac arrest. She was revived and transferred to another hospital. Once there, doctors discovered that there was a puncture hole under her armpit and also an air bubble. It was decided that it was probably due to an accidental injection. Because Kayley was transferred to the other hospital, she did survive.

Allitt's next victim was five-month-old Paul Crampton. He had been admitted for a minor infection. The nurse was not actually on duty when he was admitted but after she took over, Paul's condition deteriorated. He experienced an episode of insulin shock and nearly went into a coma. The Angel of Death was the one that raised the alarm about his serious condition. Doctors were very confused about the changes in insulin levels. After a few days, Paul began to feel better and Allitt was asked by the doctor to remove his drip. Shortly after that, he became quite ill for the second time. When he started feeling better, the dad decided to take a short break from the hospital room. The nurse was once again left in charge and the baby suffered the third attack. He was transferred to another hospital. Allitt actually went with him in the ambulance. She was also the one that had suggested that the doctors test the baby's blood sugar. Thankfully, Paul survived at the other hospital. After a few weeks, his test results came back. He had actually had 43,147 milliunits of insulin in his blood. That is one of the highest levels found in a human. The only other person that had levels this high died. It was a wonder that Paul survived with Allitt as his nurse.

Next on Allitt's list was Bradley Gibson at five years old. He had pneumonia and under the care of the Angel of Death, went into cardiac arrest. It was discovered that he also had high insulin. That night, he had a heart attack but was transferred to a second hospital and was able to survive.

Yik Hung Chan was two when he came to the hospital to recover from a fractured skull from a fall. He ended up turning blue while Allitt was working. He was given oxygen, transferred to another hospital, and recovered. The nurse was not blamed though because it was thought that the fracture was behind the boy's symptoms.

Next, Beverly focused her attention on twins on two different occasions. The twins were born premature and were under her supervision. The first twin, Becky, was found to have been cold and hypoglycemic but was released that evening. Then, that night, Becky woke up in pain but a doctor just said it was colic. She died that night. That is why the second twin, Katie, came back to the hospital for observation. Katie stopped breathing a couple of times while there. Her lungs collapsed and she suffered from brain damage and was transferred to another hospital. There, it was also discovered that five of her ribs had been broken but surprisingly, she lived. Her parents were so happy that they asked Allitt to be Katie's godmother. She agreed despite Katie having to live with partial paralysis, sight and hearing damage, and cerebral palsy.

After this, there were four additional victims that also suffered from similar symptoms as the other patients over a short period of fifteen days. There was seven-year-old Michael Davidson, nine-month-old Christopher King, eight-month-old Christopher Peasgood, and seven-week-old Patrick Elstone. Patrick was oxygen deprived and became brain damaged. People were starting to get suspicious about what was going on at this hospital.

Finally, Claire Peck, age fifteen months, became Allitt's last victim. This little baby had asthma and required a breathing tube. She was only under the care of the nurse for a couple of minutes when she had a heart attack. She survived but then had a second one later, leading to her death. It was thought that her death was because of natural causes. It was later found that she had been injected with lignocaine. This drug is not administered to babies. Claire was the Angel of Death's last victim after fifty-nine days of work.

The Investigation

After the numerous number of cardiac cases in the last few months at Grantham and Kesteven Hospital, an inquiry was launched into the cause of all of them. Deaths and comas at children's hospitals are actually pretty rare; especially if they are unexplained. At this particular children's hospital, usually only one child died a year. At first, it was thought that maybe there was a virus in the air that was making the patients sicker than when they arrived. This turned out to be incorrect. The nurses on the floor, including Beverly Allitt, talked about how maybe there was a parent or some outsider sneaking in and causing harm. That was when security cameras were placed in the hospital and the staff became more careful. They were also being watched by other people that worked in the hospital.

Next, it was discovered that there was a lot of potassium in Claire's blood. The police were called into the investigation and realized that there was lignocaine in Claire's system. This drug is given to people during cardiac arrest but is never given to a baby.

It was then that the police began to suspect that all the deaths were probably not due to natural causes. In fact, there were a lot of victims that had had high levels of insulin. To figure out what was going on, the police had a secret meeting with the hospital management to talk about a possible killer. After that, information came about that Allitt had actually reported that the key to the refrigerator where the insulin was stored had gone missing.

The next thing to do was check the daily nursing logs. Coincidentally, they were missing. The pages for the time of Paul Crampton's visit had been torn out of the book. There was also another record book that was gone. The pages were actually discovered at Allitt's house. The missing records along with her presence at every incident involving the mysteriously ill children led to her arrest.

Mary Reet, one of Allitt's coworkers was actually stunned at first to hear of her arrest. She was sure that the police had made a mistake. In fact, Katie's parents wanted to protect their daughter's godmother. They hired a detective to help prove her innocence. They even let the nurse continue to babysit Katie. Other people in the United Kingdom were also shocked. There had never been a nurse that had killed patients in the country. But with the evidence that had been collected, there was definitely no mistake about who was guilty of harming thirteen or more innocent hospital patients that were all so very young.

The Arrest/Trial

The police thought that they had enough evidence to convict Allitt but she was not actually charged until several months later. When interrogated, she did not seem scared about talking to the police. She denied any wrongdoing and said that all she had been doing was caring for the ill children. She even claimed that she was not at the hospital on some of the days in question and that at the other times she had come on the scene later and that she had been trying to help like a good nurse would do. At that point, the police did not have enough evidence to convict her so they had to let her go for the time being but that still did not erase their suspicions and she was suspended from the hospital. After all, the events at the hospital were certainly suspicious. Also, the other nurses said that she never liked to pick up crying babies and that she never seemed saddened by the deaths of any of the children. Later, she was eventually arrested.

With the investigation of Allitt's Munchausen Syndrome that led her to desire attention through the suffering of various medical conditions, it was also found that she dealt with Munchausen Syndrome by Proxy. This personality disorder is very similar to Munchausen Syndrome but instead of making oneself ill, the individual makes another one ill in order to get attention. People with Munchausen Syndrome sometimes also have Munchausen Syndrome by Proxy like Allitt. In Beverly situation, when the nurse found that she was no longer getting attention for her own medical disorders, she switched to causing them because she was able to receive attention from parents and other nurses by acting like the hero for the victims when she cared for them. The victims of people with Munchausen Syndrome by Proxy are usually children because they are unable to speak up for themselves. Allitt was made out to look like a hero at times while still working at the hospital because she was caring for the children that had become seriously ill. She was even able to diagnose some of the children's ailments rather than the doctors since she had caused the illnesses. Such as in the case of Katie, the twin, Allitt was made godmother which gave her the attention she craved.

Despite her love of attention, she did not want the attention for being a criminal. She wanted what she thought was positive attention in which people pitied her since she was sick quite often.

Allitt was evaluated by medical professionals for her disorders while in jail but she never did confess to the crimes. While she was awaiting trial however, Allitt lost a ton of weight which developed into anorexia. This was just another example of the psychological problems she experienced. Because of all of her past (and now present) illnesses, she repeated her absenteeism from nursing school and only attended sixteen days of the two-month long trial.

The trial was difficult because even though the evidence pointed to her, there were no fingerprints or any eyewitnesses. Everything was circumstantial. It had taken nearly nine months to gather the evidence that had been presented in court. The police were definitely worried about what the jury would decide. The jury deliberated for six days before they made the big decision about the Angel of Death.

She was eventually charged with four counts of murder, eleven counts of attempted murder, as well as eleven counts of causing serious harm to her patients. The parents of the victims, including the police, were overjoyed with the verdict. Justice would be served for what she had done to their children. The nurse was then given thirteen life sentences in 1993 for the murder and attempted murder of the innocent children that became her victims. Munchausen Syndrome by Proxy had no impact on the judge's decision of the extremely severe sentence that was given to Allitt. This is actually the harshest punishment ever given to a female. The judge said that he recommended that she spend at least forty years in prison before parole would even be considered but it became thirty years. As the judge said when she was sentenced, "You have turned the hospital where you worked into a killing field" (Birmingham Mail).

Allitt will be 54 in 2022 when the thirty-year possible parole could even become a possibility. It will only happen though if she has become a reformed person and is no longer a danger to herself or to anyone else. It does not change that she is still a murderer, despite having the label of Munchausen Syndrome or Munchausen Syndrome by Proxy. Though it does not seem likely that she will be released, the parents of the victims say that no matter what, they will fight back if there ever comes a chance of her leaving the prison/hospital where she is serving her time.

Prison

Allitt was sent to Rampton Secure Hospital in Nottingham to serve her sentence under the Mental Health Act. This hospital is a facility that has high security to protect prisoners suffering from mental disorders. It is not a prison because the patients/prisoners are there to receive treatment. Chris Taylor, the father of Liam Taylor, was not pleased with her placement. He thought she should be sent to jail and that it would not matter whether she killed herself in prison or not. She was sent to the hospital by the judge because of her history of self-harm. Taylor, however, looks at it as a place to take a vacation because she has a TV and is allowed to talk to other people at the hospital to form relationships with them. There is a bar and the hospital throws discos. Occasionally, Allitt has even been allowed to go out shopping as long as she is with a guard. During an interview, the former nurse mentioned that she liked the place because of the freedom it gave her that she would not receive in jail. In order for prisoners like Beverly Allitt to enjoy the freedom while receiving treatment, it costs the taxpayers of the United Kingdom £2000 a week for each inmate to stay there.2000

Her problems with Munchausen Syndrome have not ended despite being at Rampton Secure Hospital in order to receive her treatment. Once she arrived, she ate glass, stabbed herself with paperclips, and poured boiling water on her hands. On the plus side, she did admit to three of the murders and to six of the attempted ones.

Beverley was a young nurse that should have had the desire to help young children and be an advocate and a voice for them in order to heal. Growing up, she craved attention and went about negative ways to get it. She would either purposely hurt herself or lie about being ill in order to get attention. Things did not get better as she got older. Instead, she took advantage of her position at the hospital where she worked as a children's nurse. She harmed and killed many children so that she could get attention for herself. Through her attention desiring ways, she killed four children and hurt at least eleven more in the fifty-nine days that she worked as a children's nurse. Parents trusted the woman that later would become known as the Angel of Death. She will no longer be able to hurt another patient or child anymore since she has been given thirteen life sentences and will unable to be eligible for parole for at least thirty years (and that is only if she is able to show that she is no longer a danger to society).

KILLER NURSE GENENE JONES

TAMI CARLSON

Genene Anne Jones was born on July 13th , 1950 in Texas but was given up for adoption. Her adopted parents had three other children. Two were older and one was younger than Genene.

EARLY LIFE

Her adopted parents were Richard and Gladys Jones. Richard, better known as "Dick", a night club and was a gambler. He was a big spender and generous when he was flush. His club was called the Kit Kat Swim Club, the place had a dance floor with a patio and pool outside. His wife Gladys was the disc jockey at the club and the couple lived an extravagant lifestyle. They had a mansion that looked down on San Antonio, would travel often and they would both have pilot licenses .

At the age of ten, however, Genene's father was arrested for stealing the safe of a customer who had been at Jones' club at the time of the robbery. These charges were later dropped.

It could have been due to intimidation on Dick's part. The man was six feet tall, weighed a solid 240 pounds and was bold. He had an aggressive demeanor when needed and his adopted daughter developed the same traits.

His business soon failed, however. The shady Kit Kat Club soon turned into a family themed restaurant which put Dick further into debt. He then sold off the restaurant and earned a living putting up billboards around San Antonio. Genene would later describe helping her father put up the billboards as one of the happier times of her life.

Still, Genene felt as if she suffered from neglect in the adopted home. The parents had paired off the four kids on the basis of age. Genene had an older brother Wiley and an older sister named Lisa. She had a younger brother named Travis who had a learning disability that she doted on and cared for. Nonetheless, she felt jealous of all the attention that Lisa would receive. Genene referred to herself as the "black sheep" of the family and took out her frustrations on her classmates at school. She worked in the library at John Marshall and was described as "kind of bossy" by the high school librarian as she would berate other student volunteers who weren't doing their jobs up to her standards. Short and chubby, Genene felt unattractive and began to become known for lying and manipulating people.

"Lying was like talking for her," one of her classmates recalled as Genene would often tell people that she was related to Micky Dolenz, the band member of the Monkees, and that she would routinely have phone conversations with him all the time.

Tragedy would strike in her teens, however, when her younger brother Travis died in a freak accident.

He had put together a pipe bomb which exploded in his face, sending metal shards into his head. Genene took the loss hard, arriving at the funeral with a large flower wreath, crying hysterically, then feinting.

"You wonder when Genene's mind got twisted," forensic psychologist Dina Foster said. "It had to have been early on in her development when somehow, someway she got a surge of power when she was care taking for someone particularly a child. This was probably her brother, Travis. Being a caregiver for him made her feel important. She realized that she could be respected and have people look up to her until it became twisted."

A year later, her father died of cancer at the age of 56 which further devastated Genene. She had yet to graduate high school and wanted to get married. Her adopted mother refused as she Genene's choice of mate, a dropout named James "Jimmy" Harvey Delany Jr as nothing but trouble.

The two would marry, however, and live in a guesthouse near the mansion. Jimmy, however, was only interested in cars and drinking. The two would squabble often until Jimmy decided to join the Navy. With her husband away a basic training, Genene would not remain faithful, going after both single and married men. She had an affair with the newlywed husband of a former high school classmate. Then she began to tell people she had been sexually abused as a child. After four years of marriage, Genene divorced Jimmy as she stated that he had been physically abusive toward her.

Genene would threaten divorce but the two would reconcile.

"She experienced abandonment twice," Foster said. "The first go around was when her mother gave her up for adoption. The second go around was when her brothers and father died back to back. She had lost two loved ones to illnesses and one to a tragic accident. She felt helpless and out of control. But unlike most people, Genene went the criminal route in order to assuage the pain. She had to do things to get the power and control back."

CAREER LIFE & DIVORCE

Genene entered Mim's Beauty School and became a beautician, finding work at the Methodist Hospital beauty parlor. She had her first child, Richard, in 1972 while she and Jimmy were stationed in Georgia. They would move back to San Antonio but by that time the marriage was failing. She filed for divorce in Bexar County, eight months after Richard was born and stated that her husband was "a man of violent and ungovernable temper and passion" while also accusing him of "unconscionable brutality and physical cruelty." She won a court order that forbade her husband from going near both her or baby Richard. Two months later, however, the couple had gotten back together and the judge threw out the divorce suit.

"Clearly they had an on and off again relationship," Foster said. "Jimmy was hapless, wanting to do nothing more than race cars and party. So in some aspects Genene had found her soul mate, a man who needed taking care of."

But on June 3rd, 1974, Genene filed for divorce again and the couple would battle in the court system for three more years. She would file suit against Delany for failure to pay child support and in August of 1976 she won a contempt citation against him. In March of 1977, both consented to drop the legal battle and in July 17 of 1977 Genene's second child, Heather, was born. She later admitted that Heather had been conceived out of wedlock when she and Delany had another brief coming to terms.

Genene would then move back in with her adopted mother who helped with the babies as she began her training at San Antonio Independent School District's School of Vocational Nursing. Genene was a mediocre high school student but she excelled in the program, earning high grades. She aced the licensing exam and got a job at Methodist Hospital.

Genene only lasted eight months, however, getting fired when she made decisions about patient care in which she had no authority as well as being rude to patients. Genene would later claim that she was fired for standing up to a doctor who was being rude to a patient.

"She was a compulsive liar when she was a kid," Foster said. "And the lying continued into her adult life as it turned into full blown denial. She was never at fault for anything. It was always someone else, doctors, nurses, her mother, her husband. She never lived in the land of responsibility."

REIGN OF TERROR BEGINS

Genene then found work at Bexar County Hospital (now known as the University Hospital of San Antonio) where she was assigned to the Pediatric ICU.

It is here where the trouble officially began.

Her first patient had a fatal stomach disease called necrotizing enterocolitis and the boy died after surgery. Genene did not handle it well, crying hysterically. "She just went berserk," Cherylyn Pendergraft said, the RN that was orienting Genene during this time. Genene went so far as to move a stool toward the baby's cubicle and just sat there staring at the body.

Pendergraft felt the gesture odd considering that Genene had barely cared for the child.

Nonetheless, Genene saw herself as an equal to the RN's on duty and worked extra hard to acquire more knowledge than an ordinary LVN.

She worked the graveyard shift upon hire then transferred to the swing shift where she worked f3 p.m to 11 p.m while frequently volunteering for overtime and extra shifts.

Genene soon took on a reputation as the "nurse who cried wolf" to the many resident doctors who were training at the hospital. She would issue warnings about a child's worsening condition to the intern. If the intern did nothing she would then go to the resident doctor. If that physician did nothing then she would go higher up the chain of command and wouldn't stop until her recommendations were addressed.

Despite her eagerness to be perceived as on the same level as a registered nurse, Genene would skip continuation classes on the proper use of pharmaceuticals. In her first year, she was written up on eight separate occasions for giving the wrong dosage.

Genene wouldn't let any reprimands stop her, however, as she soon became the ward bully in the cramped quarters of the pediatric ICU. She would intimidate other nurses with her coarse demeanor, making more than a few transfer out of the unit to get away from her.

Her bullying tactics enabled her to make the unit her own, as she was the foul-mouthed Queen of the ward, bragging about her sexual escapades and making inappropriate remarks.

"Here we see the beginnings of tacit approval," Foster said. "No one at the hospital wants to put themselves on the line to stand up against her. It is an environment where everyone is trying to cover their own ass. No one wants to play snitch even when this woman is saying and doing all of these inappropriate things."

Even more disturbing is that Genene would also predict which baby would die.

During "report", a time in which the nurses would describe the conditions of their patients during the shift change handover to the next nurse, Genene would play the role of the Grim Reaper.

"This patient is really bad," she'd say forewarning the nurse, or even predicting death." This patient isn't going to make it."

By 1981, Genene would always demand to be assigned to the sickest patients. She seemed to enjoy the adrenaline rush of the code blues and would grieve when the child expired. Genene would hold the dead bodies and sing to it, making sure she would be the one to take the corpse to the morgue.

"She had a twisted hero complex," Foster said. "She thought of herself as equal to any RN. Most LVNs defer to the registered nurses out of education and experience. But it was quite the opposite with Genene. When the shit hit the fan she would be the first to come to the rescue. The problem was that she created these situations where she could be seen as the hero. Remember she didn't give them enough medication to kill them outright. She gave the babies just enough of a dose so that they would go into cardiac arrest. She wanted to be seen as the savior to the parents of the children she was killing. She wanted to be seen as the hero of the ward. This need was so deep-seated that she was willing to kill to get that need met. That need to be seen as a hero. That need to be seen as the most compassionate of all."

TOO MANY PATIENTS DYING

Co-workers became concerned that a surprising number of patients under the care of Jones were dying.

"The other nurses became concerned," said Vincent J.M. Dimaio, the chief medical examiner at the time. "That there were increased numbers of cardiopulmonary arrests on the ward. All her victims were children. The most innocent of the population. This would not have happened if the cases had been reported to the medical examiner's office."

Unlike most hospitals, Bexar County didn't lock their medications in a cabinet. When it become apparent that children were dying in the unit from non-fatal illnesses, the hospital dragged its feet in an investigation. There was a two-week period where seven children died in the unit. These deaths occurred only when Genene Jones was on duty and the patients were under her care.

"Astonishing," Foster said. "The tacit approval now extended to the cover up of children being murdered. The hospital administrators put their own public relations and jobs above the lives of children. It is a travesty of justice that no one at the hospital was ever punished for this."

Genene had an ally in the department in the form of Dr. James Robotham, however. Known as "JR", a reference to the ruthless businessman from the TV show Dallas, Robotham was an aggressive doctor throughout his tenure in the ICU. He had no problem dressing down nurses or student doctors who were not up to snuff or did not bend to his will. He had no hiring authority in the hospital but took on a vital role throughout the ICU by placing the patient's care onto his shoulders.

Genene saw a kindred spirit in Robotham and the doctor took a liking to her. There was one occasion in which he needed assistance and chose Genene over another nurse.

"She had been validated," Foster said. "She also wanted to be acknowledged for her nursing talents and finally there was someone who came along and anointed her as someone who was worthy."

"Robotham's Pet" as some of the nurses would later call her, would nonetheless display a macabre interest when a child came in with a fatal illness. Genene would make it clear that she wanted to be on hand when death inevitably came.

Genene would enjoy calling the parents to inform them of their child's death, sharing in their grief over the phone.

"She was Jekyll and Hyde," Foster said. "With the nurses and staff she would be coarse, demanding and condescending. But with the parents of the children she turned into the ultimate caregiver. Soft-spoken, compassionate, and joining them in their pain. She would have the parents believing that she was the most caring person on the face of the earth."

Never mind the fact that she would orchestrate the medical emergency of the child.

"That was her way of getting attention," Dimaio said. "She was a 'big person'. She was a 'big person' when she resuscitated children. When she brought them back from death's door. And the rest of her life, she wasn't anything."

THE KILLINGS MOUNT

A six month old baby named Jose Antonio Flores came into the unit with non-fatal symptoms: fever, vomiting and diarrhea. Unfortunately, he came under the care of Genene.

The baby soon suffered a seizure went into cardiac arrest and died.

Genene grabbed the dead baby and ran out of the department with the staff having to track down the crying LVN. The infant was later blood-tested and the results revealed that there had been an overdose of heparin, an anti-coagulant.

No one had ordered that the drug be administered and now the staff became suspicious.

When questioned about the baby's death, Genene resorted to manipulation and blackmail. She told the staff that she took records on every child that had died there and she knew which doctor had killed them.

Finally, one of the doctors informed the hospital administration what he suspected of Genene Jones. He had found a book in her possession about how to inject heparin through the skin without leaving a mark.

The hospital administrators, however, did not want the bad public relations fall out that would result from being a hospital that had a reputation for infant deaths.

"Say that they expected one (death) a week," Dimaio said. "All of a sudden they were getting three or four or five a week. I don't think there was any doubt that they had a good idea of what she (Genene) was doing."

"The amazing thing here is that even after the incident with the Flores' baby, Genene was allowed to continue working on the ward," Foster said.

Another child came into Genene's unit, this time to recover from open heart surgery. The child made progress but during Genene's shift he died.

"They notice that all of them (the deaths) were on the same shift," Dimaio said. "And all of them involved patients being taken care of by Genene Jones."

More doctors complained and a committee was set up to investigate. Head nurse Pat Belko and James Robotham were in charge on the hospital end but an outside team of investigators came in to look at the problem.

This third party team declined to put the blame on Genene as their findings were inconclusive.

COVERING THEIR ASS

Confident of they were in the clear, the hospital reports no abnormal deaths to the county medical examiner. Still, the hospital knew that Genene Jones was responsible for the deaths.

"She was left on the ward even though they knew what was going on," Dimaio said. "Someone said why don't we just fire her? Then they said well she'll just sue us and they'll be a big scandal. There were more interested in saving their reputation and not being sued then in the life and health of these children."

In order to avoid a public relations debacle, the administration decided to replace the LVNs in the unit with registered nurses. They said they were raising the "training bar" for ICU nurses and that LVNs would no longer be needed.

"So when they adopted that policy they let her go from that unit," Dimaio said. "Let go by the way, with an excellent letter of recommendation. Even though they knew what was going on."

Genene had been suspected in the deaths of over 47 other children, the NYT noted that the administration of Bexar County Medical Center and the University of Texas Medical school had shredded over 9,000 pounds of pharmaceutical records, records that were created during the time when Jones worked there.

By doing this, these administrators effectively destroyed any evidence that would be helpful in convicting Genene Jones of more crimes. The hospital stated that the shredding of documents was "routine" and a "coincidence", but the district attorney was able to intervene when, acting on a tip from an informant, he stopped the hospital from destroying an additional 50,000 pounds of pharmaceutical and medical records. The dean of medicine at Bexar was then cited for contempt of court when it was discovered that she withheld hospital reports from the grand jury.

"This is certainly an indictment of the hospital," Foster said. "If over 47 children were murdered, than there would have to be justice. The irony here is that the hospital administrators are not that far off from Genene Jones' mindset. They lie, deny and keep things in secret. All for the sake of control. All for the sake of being perceived that they are something they are not. Genene wanted to be seen as a hero but was really a killer. The hospital wants good pr at all costs, even childcare's lives. They are scum."

THE MURDERS CONTINUE

After her release from the county hospital and with a letter of recommendation in hand, Jones found work at a pediatric physician's clinic in Kerrville, Texas.

"She ended up here in Kerrville after she left San Antonio because of all these unexplained deaths," district attorney Ron Sutton said. "Genene Jones absolutely despises me because I brought down her little self-constructed impact."

The clinic was a start-up to be run by Dr. Kathleen Holland. She only had budget for an LVN and immediately thought of Genene Jones. She had remembered Genene and had been impressed by her take-charge personality and competence.

Holland contacted the human resource office at the hospital and inquired about the availability of Genene. Holland knew about the strange rumors about Genene but was willing to overlook them as she needed someone who could bring passion to their start up.

Holland didn't know how true those weird rumors were..

"She would create these medical emergencies," District Attorney Ron Sutton said. "That only she would know to handle. Then she would look like this supreme nurse when she would take care of the emergencies that she created."

Holland's revelation began with Petti McClellan brought in her young daughter Chelsea. McClellan said that Chelsea had a "bad cold" and went into the exam room with Dr. Holland. Genene then took the young baby out of Chelsea's arms, stating that she was going to "play" with the baby so that she and the doctor could talk.

"She had an irresistible compulsion," Foster said. "Doesn't matter where she is at, a hospital, a clinic, she has that compulsion. She'll see the opportunity to be a create the scenario for herself and she takes it."

"The protocol for the doctor's office would be the nurse, Genene Jones, would take the baby into a separate room just she and the baby, to perform whatever cursory examination; weight, blood pressure, whatever," Sutton said. "But during the time Genene would have these children by themselves all of a sudden they would become like a rag doll. And then she would scream out 'the baby's not breathing.'"

Moments later, Genene would cry out for help, saying that the baby couldn't breathe.

Doctor Holland immediately jumped into action, seeing that the baby had gone into a seizure. The child would be transported to a hospital and her life was spared.

The McClellan's expressed their gratitude toward Holland and Genene. They thought the world of the duo, believing that they saved the life of their child.

Little did they know that Genene had injected the child with succinylcholine.

Genene had used various methods to kill children under her care. She used injections of digoxin, heparin and later succinylcholine to cause a "code blue" in her patients. She would revive them afterward and receive praise. The succinylcholine she used is a paralytic that causes a temporary paralysis of skeleton muscles which can affect a patient's breathing. When she injected small children with this drug, the victim would suffer from cardiac arrest.

Petti would later return to the clinic months later with Chelsea. She had actually called the clinic to make an appointment for her son Cameron but Holland insisted that she bring Chelsea in so that she could "check on her."

"My daughter wasn't sick," Petti would later say.

Holland later disputes the claim that she asked Petti to bring Chelsea in instead of Cameron.

Unfortunately, Petti would bring Chelsea in and witness Genene administer two shots. The second shot would cause Chelsea to go into a seizure and later die.

"Once she began doing it," Foster said. "She couldn't stop. She became fueled by the adrenaline. The rush she got by sticking the syringe into the baby. The rush she got in waiting for the child to go into cardiac arrest. The the rush she got by watching the child die and comforting it in its death. She even got off on informing the parents of the baby's death. That is how twisted her mind was."

"Her original intent may not have been to kill," Foster said. "She was all about being seen as the hero, the Superwoman who came into save the day. Why she would target the same child coming in for another routine check-up really shows that she was getting careless about her victims. She had gotten away with it for so long that she didn't care. Plus, the compulsion would override whatever logic and forward thinking she had."

Chelsea's death was initially seen as sudden infant death syndrome.

"That's when we talked to the anesthesiologist," Sutton said. "He said that this child looks like it was coming out from the effects of succinylcholine, and we launched our investigation at that point."

"Soon as she got that first shot," Petti McClellan said, "Chelsey immediately starting reacting to it. And I asked her right off the bat, 'what did you do? What did you do? Something's wrong with her.'".

Genene visited Chelsey's grave and seemed genuinely remorseful.

"She was a psychopath with conflicted emotions," Foster said. "On one hand she had this need to kill and be in control of what others thought of her, specifically as a hero. And the other hand, she may have felt remorse when her 'heroic' efforts didn't produce the results she wanted."

Chelsey's mother, Petti, however, was shocked to see Genene at her daughter's grave.

Holland would later find puncture marks in a bottle of succinylcholine in a storage cabinet that only she and Genene had access to. "There were two holes in the lid of this bottle," Sutton said. "One where she had withdrawn and then she attempted to replace it with saline solution."

With the investigators closing in, Genene began to panic. She arrived at the clinic after lunch and complained to Holland that she was feeling ill…She had overdosed on her anti-depressants and began looking lethargic.

Holland immediately called the paramedics and Genene's stomach was pumped. Later upon her release, Texas Ranger Joe Davis interrogated her about the holes in the bottle of succinylcholine. Genene denied involvement, stating that she would be willing take a polygraph test.

The next day, Holland was shocked to see Genene report for work as if nothing had happened. She then informed Genene that her services would no longer be needed. Genene grew enraged and challenged Holland to take a polygraph. She then stormed out of the office.

Genene would later call back to the office and informed Holland's secretary that she had left a letter for the physician in her drawer.

The letter was a one page suicide note that she had written before she had taken the overdose of anti-depressants.

"There isn't anyway to explain to you why things are going to change. Sometimes, as wrong as it may seem, you have to except what life dishes out.

When your older, and I know your tired of hearing that, but you will be able to understand why, why I have to go away. It doesn't mean I don't love you. Please believe that. No amount of money or worldly goods could every buy my love. It is so deep & strong, it will last for all eternity.

Please explain if you can to Heather & Michael how much I love them. It's such a strong love, I can't put it on paper. I know I'm asking a lot, but I really feel your the only one who could do it.

I'm not guilty of murder, & I hope you believe that. But Daddy's way is right. It takes all the pressure off you and the seven people whose life I have altered.

No one can hurt me with my Daddy. He'll straighten this whole thing out & then we'll go home & everything will be alright. No more problems for you, no more nightmares for me.

Please make sure Michael and Heather are not separated. I know how my mother feels about Heather, but I also know how she feels about Michael. If Debbie or you can't take them together, please be sure whoever does are good people. People with lots of love.

Please don't be angry. I'm going with Daddy because I miss him and I want to be with him. He'll take care of both of us.

You'll be fine. Please believe that.

I love you,

Genene

Genene had attempted to frame Holland for the murders but all evidence pointed to her. All said and done, Genene had poisoned at least six children at the clinic. Three of the parents continued to utilize Holland as their pediatrician while three other families sued both Holland and Genene Jones as they believed that Holland knew or should have known about Genene's murderous ways.

The criminal investigation began and Chelsea's body was exhumed, revealing traces of the succinylcholine.

Her exact numbers of victims remain unknown as hospital officials first "misplaced" then destroyed records of her activities to prevent lawsuits after Genene's first conviction.

Genene would go on trial on January 15th, 1984 for the murder of Chelsea and injury to the other children. On February, 15, 1984, Genene was convicted of murder after a three hour deliberation. She was given the maximum sentence of ninety-nine years. In October, she went on trail for injuring Rolando Jones with an injection of heparin. She was sentenced a total of 159 years with the possibility of parole that came up after serving ten years.

In 1985, Gene was sentenced to 99 years in prison for killing fifteen month old Chelsea McClellan.

Later that year, she was sentenced to a term of sixty years in prison for the attempted murder of Rolando Jones with heparin.

"I've had several cases that stand out in my mind," Sutton said. "But this one is particularly heinous because of death to small children.

SERIAL KILLER TO BE RELEASED

Genene Jones is now set to go free because of a legal loophole in the form of She is now scheduled for mandatory release in February 2018 due to a Texas law that prevents prison overcrowding. Genene has been a prisoner who has exhibited "good behavior", becoming eligible for the release.

"Please, please, please, do not let this person walk," Petti McClellan said.

"Genene Jones is probably one of the worst types of serial killers because keep in mind who her victims were," said Andy Kahan, a victim advocate. "Defenseless, voiceless, babies. One of the nation's most diabolical serial killers in our country's history is set to be legally released,"

"I was so angry that it went on for so long," Cherlyn Pendergraft said. "That so many children had to die."

Jones now claims to be sickly and is housed in medical jail unit.

"Am I prepared that she walks?" McClellan asked. "No. Because she's gonna hurt another child. I don't want to hear that she's sick. Or that she's old, she's two years older than I am."

"There is absolutely no reason for Genene Jones to be walking the streets," Foster said. "She has a compulsion that has to be satiated. She needs to be locked up for the rest of her life."

The current District Attorney is looking to re-open old cases against Jones in order to keep her in prison.

NIELS HOEGEL

CHRIS HAMPTON

Niels Hoegel

"Apparently some of his colleagues already called him bad luck charm because very often he was already around when a patient needed to be resuscitated so they just thought...you know...just by chance...he's around and he helps assist junior doctors but from what I've heard people suspected, there were suspicions, there were rumours but nothing...no evidence...nothing concrete."

Uli Hesse, Journalist.[1]

An Inconspicuous Beginning

Not much is known about the private life of Niels Hoegel, the life he led before he was catapulted (or rather catapulted himself) into the spotlight. But Niels Hoegel appeared to be a caring, compassionate man who seemed destined to spend his life helping other people.

Hoegel was born in Wilhelmshaven on December 30th, 1976. German reporting rules have kept most of the details of his personal life away from the public eye, but what is known is that Hoegel's father was also a nurse, at the Willehad Hospital. [2] His mother was a paralegal, and his older sister was a dentist – to all intents and purposes the entire Hoegel family was dedicated to helping others. His parents separated when Niels was just 11 years of age – a situation which he found difficult to handle. His ambition had always been to be a firefighter – however, this was never going to come to fruition because Hoegel suffered from acrophobia or a fear of heights.[3]

He was educated at the IGS (comprehensive school) in Wilhelmshaven, where his friends and former teachers remember him as a 'normal' student, widely accepted and fairly popular. He is described as funny and helpful, although his teachers made a point of remarking that he was less than engaged in class. While at school it appeared that the young Niels Hoegel was more interested in football than his studies, something which was borne out by the fact that he never graduated. When asked to describe him as a student, one teacher remarked that *"he was a fairly normal student".*

Hoegel was apparently less than forthcoming with the girls and was not the type to have the confidence to approach them in the school yard.

However, what he lacked in romantic aptitude he more than made up for in his medical studies, showing a predilection for medicine, giving his father high hopes that his son would go on to become a doctor. Perhaps it was his failure to live up to his father's expectations which planted the 'God Complex' in his mind – the complex which would take the lives of many people in the following years.

Niels Hoegel, the Nurse

When he was 17, Hoegel began his nursing studies at St Willemad Hospital, where he discovered the joys of alcohol, drugs, and members of the opposite sex, a time he described as 'the best phase of his life.'[3] However, once again his former friends and fellow students remember him as just being 'nice'. There was nothing remarkable or notable about the young man – he was just 'normal'.[4]]

After graduation, Hoegel took up a position at the Oldenburg Clinic on June 15th, 1999. For the first few weeks Hoegel, like all new staff, was accompanied by a senior member of staff.[5] The clinic was known as an excellent hospital, in particular with regards to its heart surgery intensive care unit. However, Niels Hoegel found himself floundering slightly under the stressful atmosphere and pressured conditions which a heart surgery center naturally entails. So stressful was it, in fact, that Hoegel described his first cardiac surgery as *a "traumatizing experience"*. The effect on Hoegel was quite profound – he began to drink heavily and developed depression and anxiety.[6]

Things soon started to go wrong at the exemplary Oldenburg hospital. As the death rate of patients began to rise, so did the rumours. Hoegel's fellow nurses noticed that this increase in deaths coincided with his arrival at the clinic, but despite the whisperings around the hospital, nothing was officially noted. Without any firm evidence, the hospital decided not to go to the police - they felt that they could not take 'gut feelings' and suspicions to the authorities.[7]

Suspicions grew, and in August 2001 a meeting of doctors and nurses from the clinic was held to discuss the situation, a meeting which Niels Hoegel himself attended. It was pointed out that, whenever Hoegel was on duty, the number of deaths and/or the need for resuscitation was higher. Hoegel, of course, denied the allegations and following the meeting he took three weeks off work, claiming sickness. It was noted that, during his absence, only two patients died – much less than the figure which had become the norm during Hoegel's shifts.[8]

Hoegel returned to work in mid-September after his leave of absence and began working on the night shift. Once again the number of unexplained deaths rose. Almost straight away five patients become inexplicably ill, needing to be resuscitated an overall total of ten times. All five patients died – three immediately, and the remaining two a short time later. It had now become blindingly obvious that Niels Hoegel was behind the deaths – 58% of deaths at the hospital occurred under his care.[9] In September 2002 he was given the option to either resign or move to a more 'mundane' position within the hospital. Hoegel resigned. On October 10th, 2002, the nursing director of the Oldenburg hospital gave Hoegel a glowing reference, despite her full knowledge of the suspicions surrounding his conduct while working at her hospital. In the reference, her claims included terms which suggested that Hoegel had been a valuable member of staff, stating that he had worked *"prudently, conscientiously and independently…in a critical way and has acted correctly"* and that he displayed *"willingness to serve, and cooperative behavior".* In conclusion, she stated that *"he had completed the tasks assigned to him to the fullest satisfaction".*[10]

That reference sealed the fate of many patients who would be unfortunate to find themselves under Niels Hoegel's care in the coming months and years.

Delmenhorst

In 2003 Niels Hoegel moved to Delmenhorst, and a year later, in 2004, he got married. That same year his wife gave birth to a little girl. The birth, by all accounts, was a difficult one, even life threatening for the baby and Hoegel was forced to stand by and watch, unable to do a thing to help.[11] Could this helplessness have acted as a trigger? It certainly seems possible, likely even, because, in the months which followed, many more lives would be lost at the hands of Niels Hoegel.

Home for Hoegel and his family was a quiet residential area called Ganderkesee, an unassuming area midway between the city and the countryside. It was a good place in which to raise a family – people weren't afraid to go out at night, and there were plenty of families with children living close by. The Hoegel residence was a small semi-detached house, with space for parking, and a garden in which Hoegel's daughter could play.

Life was typically suburban. Niels would talk to his neighbors over the garden fence, passing the time of day and exchanging pleasantries with them. When one of his neighbors was pregnant, Hoegel kept a watchful eye on her and helped to look after her.[12] It was comforting to know there was a nurse living close by, someone the neighbors could go to for help if needed.

But there was another side to Hoegel, one that sometimes showed its face to the neighbors. Whenever the subject of an accident, for instance, came up Hoegel would make sarcastic comments about the victims, in direct contrast to the caring, compassionate nurse most people thought he was.[13]

Family life overwhelmed Hoegel, and he threw himself into his work, even choosing to spend his free time working for the Red Cross Ambulance Service rather than spending his time at home with his wife and daughter. Life was spiralling out of control, and he began to drink and take drugs more heavily.[14]

Towards the end of 2002, Hoegel found himself a new position, this time at the intensive care unit at Delmenhorst hospital.[15]

"He seemed to have been pretty unassuming...blended in in a way but obviously he had also this other side...that he wanted to show off his skills, but in a way, he seemed to be pretty relaxed and just a colleague for most of them."]

Following a car accident, although uninjured Hoegel began to take medication for the panic attacks which began soon afterwards. His substance abuse didn't go unnoticed among his colleagues.

"Alcohol, his medication, and even more work. It seems he also defined himself a lot about his job and about his work...so maybe that was one of the reasons he needed this feeling of being a hero."[16]

Intensive care was the perfect environment for Niels Hoegel.

"Patients in intensive care are the sickest patients in the hospital so there is a higher death rate there than there would be from a normal ward. So a higher death rate would not necessarily spark suspicions unless it was out of keeping with previous years or other intensive care units."[17]

Hoegel found himself once again at the center of staff room suspicions. It was already well known that the nurse was a heavy drinker and was becoming more and more reliant on prescription medications, but his colleagues were also curious as to why this highly skilled nurse had left his previous position at Oldenburg.

But that wasn't all. His behaviour was arousing suspicion about his professional conduct within Delmenhorst itself. Hoegel always seemed to be present when there was a patient in need of resuscitation, and it became something of a standing joke that he was a bad luck charm – bringing death to his patients whenever he was on duty. But, just as was the case with Oldenburg, nothing was done about the suspicions.

Until Hoegel got careless.

"He was only caught by chance. We assume that he injected a patient on the intensive care unit...with the heart drug. And we know that a nurse came into the room just when the patient went into cardiac arrest, and

somehow she was a little bit...something wasn't quite right, so she helped resuscitate the patient, and afterwards checked and she found five vials of this particular heart drug in one of the wastebaskets on the intensive care unit. She didn't know that he had just injected a patient who was stable with this particular heart drug and he fell into a cardiac arrest. The nurse realized that he needed to be resuscitated. She did this...a colleague helped her...but she was kind of suspicious. She found the entire situation very strange because the patient had been stable. So she talked with her colleague and her colleague found, also by chance, empty vials of this particular heart drug in a wastebasket on the intensive care unit. And that's how it all started."

The empty vials had contained a drug called Ajmalin, an antidysrhythmic drug which is used to slow down the heart rate of a patient whose heart is beating at an abnormally high rate. Hoegel's victims, however, had normal heart rates, so when they received the Ajmalin, their heart would slow to a dangerously low level, often resulting in cardiac arrest.

The suspicious nurse took her concerns to her colleagues.

The patient in question was in intensive care suffering from lung cancer and had no heart issues which would have necessitated the use of the drug.

Arrest

This time the suspicions were taken seriously, and Niels Hoegel was arrested and charged but incredibly he was allowed to continue working. With no prior suspicions against him (that they were aware of) the authorities believed it was a one off, a mistake perhaps, or a momentary lapse in judgement. The case was treated as one of negligence, rather than homicide.

The case went to trial, and in 2008 nurse Niels Hoegel was found guilty of one charge of manslaughter and was sentenced to seven and a half years.

And there it might have remained, had a woman who had been following the case not come forward.

"A woman heard about that story, and she went to the police because she suspected that her late mother was also killed by Niels, and that started a whole new investigation."[18]

Brigitte Arndt

On March 27th, 2003, Kathrin Lohmann waved goodbye to her 61-year-old mother, Brigitte Arndt, and left the Delmenhorst hospital to return home. It had been a worrying time for Kathrin – her mother had been seriously ill, but now the tide seemed to have turned and, having survived a coma, Brigitte was now on the mend and was looking forward to being discharged from hospital and going home with her daughter to her house in Berne.

But as Kathrin left the hospital she was overcome with a dreadful feeling of foreboding – a feeling that that would be the last time she saw her mother alive. She shook it off and went home.

Later on that evening, Kathrin called the hospital, as she did every night, to check on her mother's condition and to reassure herself that all was well. Something about the male's voice on the other end of the phone worried Kathrin, but nevertheless, she went to bed, safe in the knowledge that had there been anything of concern, the nurse would have told her.

But she was to hear that same male voice only a few hours later when the phone rang at 1.30 am, telling her that Brigitte's condition had deteriorated and that she needed to return to the hospital immediately.

Kathrin was met at the hospital by two doctors, who told her that, despite their best efforts, her mother had passed and that they had done all they could for her. Standing in the corridor, Kathrin cried and screamed for her mother.

Kathrin was filled with remorse. It had been at her own insistence that her mother had gone to the hospital in the first place – perhaps if she had not persuaded her to seek help she would still be alive. But her feelings of guilt slowly changed to doubt – doubt that her mother's death had been natural, doubt that the staff at the hospital had really done all they could for Brigitte. But there was nothing she could do – friends and family slowly drifted away, doubting her claims, and Kathrin's life went downhill. She slipped into a deep depression, and, unable to work she was forced to move into a one room apartment in a less than desirable area.

And that was her life, until five years later when she saw the story of Nurse Niels Hoegel's conviction for murder on the news.

She knew she had been right. She received no support from family and friends, who could not believe that she was going back over her mother's death again, but she was determined to get the truth about Brigitte, so she took her story to the police in Delmenhorst.

They looked into it, and found, to their interest, that Hoegel had been on duty in intensive care the night Brigitte had died. Kathrin pushed for answers and asked repeatedly for her mother's body to be exhumed. She came up against some strong opposition – the public prosecutor's office told her time and time again that exhumations were too expensive, but she persisted.

In spring 2009 Kathrin got her wish. Brigitte Arndt's grave, at Warfleth cemetery in Wesermarsch, was surrounded with covers as an excavator dug up her coffin, and her remains were taken away for examination. Once again, Kathrin was by herself, both emotionally and physically. There was no priest there to bless the body, and the grave was waterlogged from the nearby dyke. Kathrin wondered if she had disturbed her mother's body for nothing – she was afraid the water might have washed away what little evidence there might be.

She had a long wait, but finally, after many more calls to the prosecutor's office, Kathrin had her answer. Traces of Ajmalin, which is found in the drug Gilurytmal, was discovered in Brigitte's system. Niels Hoegel had murdered her mother.[19]

More Horror

Following Kathrin Lohmann's suspicions and the subsequent proof that Niels Hoegel had murdered her mother, police prepared for the mass exhumation of many more bodies.

When questioned about Brigitte's murder, Hoegel admitted his guilt.

"He made the police's life quite easy by admitting to having killed people in the past. Now, these kinds of killers don't just admit things because they feel remorse or because they're sorry for what they've done. He would have seen some benefit to him in admitting it. He probably recognized that the game was up and that it would be beneficial to him in terms of [a] shortened sentence or the amount of attention he might receive, to admit it."

Hoegel's admission was not as straightforward as it seemed. By causing his patients to crash, and then bringing them back, or attempting to bring them back, to life, Hoegel was always in the limelight, ever the hero. And his confession to the police about having killed more patients only served to keep the attention on him.

"Having admitted that he had killed people, he kind of threw down the gauntlet to the police. He'd made it easy in one way but made it very difficult in another way because he wouldn't give them any details and he was saying that he couldn't remember, and his story kept changing, which is a tactic often used by these kinds of people to keep the attention on themselves. So the police then had to go and get the hard evidence to be able to take him to court, and unfortunately, that meant exhuming a lot of the bodies to see if there were drugs in their system. Many of the bodies had been cremated so this wasn't actually possible."

Traces of the same drug which Hoegel had used on Brigitte Arndt were found in 14 exhumed bodies.

In 2015, Niels Hoegel was convicted of three counts of murder, and two of attempted murder. At his trial, he had the attention he craved so much, but it was the wrong kind of attention.

"When he was brought in Niels H hid his face with a folder, and that wasn't remorse, that was probably because he doesn't like negative attention. This man has spent most of his adult life, it would seem, craving positive attention from being a hero. He's not being perceived as a hero at the moment and he would find that very difficult to deal with."

The police had strong suspicions that there were more victims than they had discovered, but while their investigations continued they satisfied themselves that Hoegel would be convicted for the deaths they could so far prove.

"While he was on trial, he started to talk with a forensic psychiatrist...a court appointed forensic psychiatrist, and this psychiatrist had already the feeling that he wanted to confess something. And he did. He told him that he injected this particular heart drug to 90 more patients at that hospital alone, and of those 90 patients, about 30 died. That was a big shock of course...so they started to exhume bodies."

Yet more bodies were exhumed – more heartache for many more families as their deceased loved ones were disturbed. Of course, this is exactly what the narcissistic Niels Hoegel wants, to keep himself in the spotlight, getting the attention he so desired.

"So, they had this massive investigation, they went through hundreds of medical records and looking for clues, because they couldn't just dig up hundreds of bodies and they realized that there were about 285 patients who had died during or shortly after his shifts. And of those 285, 101 were cremated and 184 were still buried. So, they went through their records again and they decided to dig up 99, and of those 99 I believe 27 showed traces of the heart drug he used."

The forensic psychiatrist had his work cut out for him. Niels Hoegel couldn't remember, or claimed he couldn't remember, any details of his victims, details which the police needed in order to further their investigations. Whether that was a ruse on Hoegel's part to perpetuate the attention, or whether he genuinely couldn't remember, is anybody's guess. The forensic psychiatrist had to work tirelessly in order to glean the necessary information from Hoegel.

He 'regressed' Hoegel to his time at the hospital, uncovering tiny details in order to stimulate his memories – details such as positioning of the beds, the windows, his signature on the medical records – anything which might bring Hoegel's mind back to each crime.

"He confesses to the 27 deaths they found in principal because he can only remember a few details which is very very odd but also if he has killed so many people, maybe, you know, you just don't remember all the details anymore."

Escalation

There is a phenomenon among serial killers known as the cooling off period, and at first Hoegel's cooling off period – that is, the time between killings -would last months. Criminologist Jane Monckton-Smith explains:

"When we talk about serial killers and the cooling off period, what we're talking about is their compulsion to kill, so the compulsion slowly gets stronger and stronger, if you think of it like a graph until we get to the peak, where they feel they need to kill, and they do that. And then they feel satiated and they start to come back down again, and this is why we see with serial killers quite a lot, that they can just return to normal after they have killed somebody, and we can't understand that...so while they're in this period of having cooled off, it starts to build again, and build again, and when it does build again they will be compelled to kill when they hit the top of that peak, and in this case it seemed that his need to kill was getting shorter and shorter, and so he was needing to kill more and more often."[20]

But was Ajmalin the only drug used by Hoegel in his killing spree? The police think not. On studying the number of deaths, it was found that he was suspected of killing more than once per shift – there were 50 double deaths (meaning two deaths occurred on one shift) and nine triple deaths (three deaths in one shift). Hoegel was present at 92% of the double deaths, and at all of the triple deaths and yet, Ajmalin could only be found in six of these cases, leading investigators to believe that the homicidal nurse employed more than one method of murder.[21] Police have pinpointed 5 different drugs which they say Hoegel used – Ajmalin, Lidocaine, Calcium Chloride, Amiodarone and Solatol, all of which cause heart arrhythmia and low blood pressure.

And So it Goes On

Hoegel is still being investigated, despite having already been jailed for life. As more and more evidence is uncovered, the story unfolds even more.

It is now believed that Hoegel first murdered a patient in February 2000, when he was still working at the Oldenburg clinic. It is also believed that he went on to kill around 35 more patients at the clinic before moving to Delmenhorst, where he was free to continue the stealthy slaughter of his patients. As the investigation into Nurse Niels Hoegel's crimes is set to continue, nobody knows how many patients he killed while pretending to care for them, although it is thought to be at least 90.

Hoegel isn't the only person to be held accountable for these deaths, however. Six members of staff from the Delmenhorst clinic are facing charges of manslaughter for their failure to intervene, and it seems likely that staff at Oldenburg Hospital will also be made to face the consequences of their inactions.

Remorse

A psychiatrist involved in the case told the court that Hoegel was full of remorse for the pain he had inflicted on the bereaved families, and, contrary to popular belief he was not 'basking in the limelight' of the case. "*This is not so. He is deeply ashamed,*" [22]

But there are others who doubt his sincerity.

"*He has expressed his remorse, he said he is honestly sorry for what he did, he hopes the families will find peace for the crimes he committed.*

But...he also said that it happened relatively spontaneous, which doesn't sound like taking on a lot of responsibility."[23]

As the German judicial system does not hand down consecutive sentences, any further convictions will not affect Hoegel's sentence[24], but it may bring some small relief to those families who have been in limbo, not knowing whether their loved ones died of natural causes or if they were, in fact, murdered.

Nurse Niels Hoegel craved attention – and that attention seems set to continue for many years to come.

SEE JANE KILL : THE GREATEST FEMALE SERIAL KILLER

AMY DEMPSEY

Jane Toppan

In 1887, a woman named Amelia Phinney was recovering from surgery for a uterine ulcer at Cambridge Hospital, Boston. Suffering pain from the procedure, she asked her nurse for something to ease the discomfort. The nurse, Jane Toppan, obliged, and although the medicine she gave to Amelia tasted foul, Jane encouraged her to finish it. As she drifted in and out of consciousness, she felt someone in the bed with her, kissing her face and caressing her. The attention suddenly stopped, and the following morning Amelia awoke and put the memories down to a strange dream. It wasn't until 1901, when Jane Toppan was arrested, that Amelia realised she had escaped the Angel of Death.

Her Early Years

Jane Toppan was born in Boston, Massachusetts, in 1857. Records about her early life are few and far between, but it is known that she was born Honora Kelley, the youngest of three daughters [2] (although some records show two daughters, and others suggest four) to Irish immigrants, Peter and Bridget Kelley. Bridget died of consumption (tuberculosis) when Honora was small, and Peter was left to raise his daughters alone. However, Peter was a chronic drunk. Known locally as 'Kelley the crack' (crackpot) for his eccentric and erratic drunken behaviour, [3] he was unable to cope with his daughters and in 1863 Peter placed his two youngest daughters, Honora and Delia, into the Boston Female Asylum, [4] an orphanage for orphans and destitute girls in Boston. [5]

When staff at the orphanage saw the poor state of the girls, they agreed to take them in. Peter Kelley later succumbed to insanity and was institutionalised for, allegedly, sewing his own eyelids together whilst working as a tailor. An older daughter, Nellie, was also reportedly institutionalised when she went violently insane in her twenties. [6]

The Toppans

In 1865, when Honora was only 7 or 8, she was taken in by the Toppan family as an indentured servant, meaning that she worked in service in return for bed, board, education and an agreed sum to be paid at the age of 18 when she would be released from her contract.

Although the family never formally adopted Honora, she took their last name and changed her first name to Jane. [8]

Jane excelled at school. She was described as 'brilliant and aggressive, and a leader of her class. She was also troubled, resorting to petty theft and lying. [9]

Jane's foster sister, Elizabeth, always treated her with kindness, but despite this, Jane's time with the Toppan family was not happy. Ann Toppan, the head of the household, treated Jane with disdain and made her feel ashamed of her Irish heritage. So much so, in fact, that she told friends that the young girl was an Italian immigrant whom the family had rescued from the streets.

Jane herself adopted this attitude, and in a bid to forget her own roots she would often be heard making disparaging remarks about other Irish people.

Ann Toppan was a cruel taskmaster and took every given opportunity to make her foster daughter feel small. As a result, Jane developed a personality which made her appear affable to others and was well-known for telling tall stories. But even this was ammunition for Mrs Toppan, as she attributed Jane's fondness for story-telling to the 'gift of the gab' – a talent for which the Irish were well-known. [10]

Despite Elizabeth's kindness, however, Jane developed an intense jealousy of her foster sister. Elizabeth was older by some years, and far prettier than 'plain Jane' and the younger girl envied Elizabeth's beauty and certain marriage.

These feelings were further compounded when, according to some reports, Jane was courted by a young man, an office worker from Lowell, when she was in her late teens. The relationship seemed to be going well when the young suitor gave Jane an engagement ring engraved with the image of a bird. Things turned sour, however, when the young man took a job in another town and fell in love with the daughter of his new landlord, and he called off the engagement. [11]

This betrayal proved to be a pivotal point in Jane's future behaviour, as she has been cited as saying "*If I had been a married woman, I probably would not have killed all of those people. I would have had my husband, my children and my home to take up my mind.*" [12] Such was Jane's misery at being jilted, she began eating for comfort and gained a considerable amount of weight – at one point reaching 170lbs, which, on a diminutive 5'3" frame, is a lot of weight to carry. Her feelings of worthlessness grew, along with her resentment of the much-courted Elizabeth.

In 1874, Jane, by now 18, was released from her indenture and paid a lump sum of $50 (roughly $1064. 73 in today's money [13]) as per the terms of her contract. However, she decided to remain at the house in service to the family. Elizabeth married a young deacon of the local church, Oramel Brigham, and shortly afterwards her mother, Ann Toppan died, leaving everything to Elizabeth and nothing to her foster daughter, [14] a fact which further cemented Jane's resentment and loathing of her foster sister.

Jane stayed at the Toppan's house for a further ten years after she was released from her indenture. She was 28 when she eventually left in 1885. Although nothing is known about the circumstances of her departure – whether she was told to leave or left of her own free will – it *is* known that the ever gracious Elizabeth told Jane that there would always be a room at the house for her, should she wish to return. [14]

Nurse Jane

When Jane left the Brigham household, she decided to go into nursing, (one of only a handful of professions available to someone of Jane's social standing and gender), and began training at Cambridge Hospital in Boston.

Nurse Jane was a firm favorite among the patients – they loved her and nicknamed her 'Jolly Jane'. Her once maligned 'gift of the gab' stood her in good stead with the patients, who found her to be warm, attentive and caring.

Her co-workers, however, saw a vastly different side to their new colleague. She quickly became known as a liar and was wont to spread rumours about her colleagues and speak ill of people behind their backs to others. The rest of the staff quickly learnt not to trust the new trainee nurse.

Her professional ethics were also called into question when she was accused of stealing, and of altering patients' charts. Of course, Jane vehemently denied these accusations, and with no proof was allowed to continue with her training. [15] In actual fact, according to some sources, Jane's behaviour towards her fellow nurses, on occasion, led to a dismissal, and far from being dismayed that her antics had caused a colleague to lose her job, Jane would exhibit such extreme pleasure at their fate that it would alarm her fellow co-workers. [16]

The Angel of Death Emerges

It was during this time at Cambridge Hospital, that Jane began experimenting with her patients. At first, she would simply tamper with the patients' charts, or administer small amounts of medicine to the ones she liked to make them sick and prolong their stay. [17] However, as time went on this didn't appear to satisfy Jane's appetite for experimentation, and she began using her patients as guinea pigs in earnest, with deadly results. The small amounts of medicine used to induce sickness were no longer enough, and Jolly Jane turned to the drugs which were to become her hallmark – morphine and atropine.

To the Brink of Death

It is believed that in the beginning at least, Jane relied solely on morphine in her experiments. She would inject her chosen patient with the drug and stand back to watch the effects. The patient's pupils would contract, their skin would become clammy, and their breathing became laborious and loud. Depending on the dosage given, some of those patients would then slip into a coma, or even just stop breathing. Most satisfying to Jane, however, was when the patient would convulse, their body contorted with pain before they died.

On more than one occasion, Jane would take her patient to the brink of death before reviving them again, gaining a sense of professional pride in her life-saving skills. However, no matter how elated she felt having saved one of her victims' lives, nothing could compare to the thrill of seeing and feeling the life slip out of her target's body.

Soon, though, Jane had to add another ingredient to her deadly arsenal – atropine. Atropine is a fatal poison, derived from the belladonna plant, and was widely used in Victorian hospitals as a painkiller, as well as a go-to drug for many other conditions, such as whooping cough and tetanus. By introducing atropine to the mix, Jane could now witness (and enjoy) an entirely new set of effects. Pupils would dilate (rather than contract, as with the morphine), and patients would lose control of their muscles, often appearing intoxicated. The results would have been spectacular and gratifying for Jane to watch – her victims would sometimes laugh maniacally, or make low groaning sounds, much like that of a wounded animal. But possibly the most satisfying and exciting manifestation for Jane would be that of her patients pulling and plucking at objects around them, whether real or otherwise. Clothing, bed covers, their own fingers and toes – they would be compelled to pick continuously, even in their final moments, right up until death.

Jane was not content with merely administering the two drugs, though. She took great pleasure and interest in varying the dosages, watching the effects of the combinations. Her usual *modus operandi* seemed to be first injecting the patient with morphine and then, as they were about to lose consciousness, would offer them a glass of water with atropine dissolved in it. Sometimes, it seems, she would wait until the patient was near death from the morphine overdose, and then administer the atropine directly into the bowel by way of an enema, thus removing the last vestiges of dignity the patient might have left.

It is worth noting that Jane knew exactly what she was doing when using these drugs. Training of a nurse at that time was rigorous, to say the least. Much of it would have been what she had been used to in her years of service to the Toppans – cleaning, dusting, scrubbing floors and general 'housekeeping' of the wards for very little money, approximately $7 per month, out of which she had to buy all her books, as well as clothes and anything else she needed. But the training also included a weekly lecture on the medical profession and would have included the correct dosage and administration of drugs, of which morphine and atropine were just two. In fact, her final exam would have included questions on the correct dosage of atropine, morphine, and what should be done if a patient overdoses.

Jolly Jane Toppan knew exactly what she was doing.

There was more than one reason for Jane to use both atropine and morphine on her victims. Her first motivation was her own amusement. Jane got a huge thrill from watching her patients' reactions. She had a sadistic lust for their suffering and gained great pleasure from watching them writhe in pain before dying.

Her other reason for using the two drugs, however, was self-preservation. By using two substances which produced diametrically opposed reactions (morphine constricts the pupils, while atropine dilates them, for example), she could confuse the doctors who would examine the patients. In the absence of any textbook symptoms, the doctors would often attribute their deaths to a heart attack or diabetes. Jane would have derived a great deal of satisfaction from not only playing God with her patients but also from confounding the doctors. [18]

Sexual Thrill

Jane's perversion didn't stop at merely watching her patients suffer and die. Whilst it is not clear whether she sexually abused her victims, she later readily admitted to experiencing a sexual thrill from watching her patients dying, and this is borne out in the fact that she would climb into bed with them when they were close to death, pull them into her arms and hold them tight as the life drained out of their bodies. [19]

It was during this time that 36-year-old Amelia Phinney had her own brush with death at the hands of Nurse Jane. Amelia had had surgery for a uterine ulcer, a procedure which involved burning the ulcer with silver nitrate, and was recovering in bed at Cambridge Hospital. The post-operative pain she was experiencing made sleep impossible, and she became aware of someone standing by her bed. In the low light of the oil lamp, Amelia Phinney recognised her nurse, Jane Toppan, whose face, she recalled, had a look of deep intensity. Amelia asked Jane to fetch a doctor, as her pain was so bad, but Jane told her there was no need for a doctor, and she gave Amelia a drink, holding her up so she could sip.

Amelia did as her nurse told her, and shortly afterwards began to lose consciousness, but she later recalled that, through the haze, she felt the bedclothes being pulled back and another body joining her in bed. That body belonged to Jane Toppan, who proceeded to whisper to Amelia that everything would be alright. Amelia was powerless to move as the nurse caressed her, kissed her face, and peered excitedly into her eyes. The glass was once again brought to Amelia's lips as the nurse gently told her to drink some more, but the patient resisted and Jane suddenly left the bed and hurried from the room as though someone had disturbed her.

The next morning, when Amelia awoke, she put the bizarre happenings from the previous night down to a dream. [20]

Moving On

Although Jane was not liked by her colleagues, she had earnt the respect of some of the doctors at Cambridge Hospital, and, in order for Jane to further her studies, in 1888, they recommended her to the Massachusetts General Hospital.

Once again, Jane proved unpopular with her fellow nurses, who accused her of giving incorrect dosages to her patients. Talk was rife, with suspicions that several patients under Jane's care had died needlessly. However, it wasn't until the summer of 1890 that Jane was fired from her post at Massachusetts General, for leaving the ward without permission - a firm rule at the time.

Jane briefly returned to her job at Cambridge Hospital, but that was short lived as she was asked to leave because of reckless administration of opiates, a reputation which had dogged her career.

Private Nurse

In the summer of 1891, Jane decided to become a private nurse, and indeed she earned a reputation as the most successful private nurse in Cambridge. Her personality was not above reproach, however – her habit of telling lies and stealing continued and caused concern among some of her employers. Her free time did nothing to quash this reputation as Jane was known for drinking, and spreading rumours in her free time.

The Murders

Jane didn't need sick patients to murder, far from it. In fact, anyone who got in the way of what she wanted fell prey to the Angel of Death.

In 1895 Jane poisoned and killed Israel Dunham, her 77-year-old landlord because he was, according to her, feeble. Again, due to the complexities of her methods, doctors attributed his death to heart failure. Jane remained at no 19, Wendell Street, Boston, with Israel's widow, Lovey. However, by 1897 Jane had grown tired of her 'old and cranky' landlady. When the old lady fell ill in September of that year,

Jane 'nursed' her, with her standard morphine and atropine. Lovey Dunham died.

1899 saw Jane claim two more victims. In the summer of that year, Jane stayed (as she had for several years) at a rented vacation home in Cataumet, Cape Cod. She had maintained a somewhat strained relationship (at least on her part) with her foster sister, Elizabeth Brigham, and that summer Jane invited Elizabeth to join her at the house. The pair had enjoyed a pleasant picnic, and on return to the house, Jane exacted her revenge. She mixed morphine with mineral water and gave it to her foster sister. However, Jane wanted Elizabeth, the foster sister she had resented for so many years, to suffer...a fact borne out years later when Jane confessed to her crimes, stating that Elizabeth was "really the first of my victims that I actually hated and poisoned with vindictive purpose." A quick death was not revenge enough for Jane, so she dragged the death out until finally, Jane climbed into bed with and held the dying woman as she took her last breath, later saying "I held her in my arms and watched with delight as she gasped her life out."

In December of that same year, a 70-year-old widow named Mary McNear was suffering from a cold and cough, having picked it up on Christmas day whilst visiting her daughter in Cambridge, who wasn't very well herself. Mary's family were concerned about her health and raised the idea of hiring a nurse to care for the elderly lady. The family's doctor, Dr Walter Wesselhoeft, however, deemed it unnecessary, saying that she only had a cold and their servant could administer everything she needed for her recovery – bed rest and hot tea. The family still felt a nurse was needed and asked Dr Wesselhoeft to recommend someone.

That someone was Jane Toppan.

Cheered and encouraged by the care and attention the nurse was bestowing on her Grandmother, Evelyn Shaw (Mary's granddaughter) returned home happy, but Mary's coachman arrived shortly after to tell her that Mary had passed out and could not be revived. Evelyn returned to her grandmother's house. The Dr was already there when she arrived and told Evelyn that Mary had suffered a stroke after receiving her medication. Nurse Toppan had informed the staff but told them there was no cause for alarm. The cook, though, took it upon herself to send the coachman to Evelyn's house despite Jane's assurances that all was well. The following morning, December 29th, 1899, Mary McNear passed away without having regained consciousness.

After the funeral, Mary's relatives discovered that some of Mary's best clothes were missing, and voiced their concerns to the doctor that the nurse may have stolen them. He, however, was furious at the suggestion and the family dropped the matter. [21]

Nothing and nobody would stand in the way of Jane getting what she wanted. February 1900 saw Jane's victimology take a new twist- the murder of a friend. Myra Connors was an old friend of Jane's and worked at the Theological School as a dining matron. Jane needed money, so she poisoned Myra with strychnine and took her job. Her position was short-lived, however, when Jane's stealing came to light and she was dismissed.

The Ones That Got away

Jane's next three victims escaped death at Jane's hands, but this was by design, and not luck on their part. In 1901, at the age of 44, Jane took up residence with new landlords, Melvin and Eliza Beedle. Never one to enjoy paying rent, Jane poisoned her landlords, but only enough to make them sick enough to need the help of a nurse. As she nursed them back to health, Jane turned her attention to the Beedle's housekeeper, Mary Sullivan. Jane poisoned Mary so that she fell unconscious and Jane brought it to the Beedle's attention that their housekeeper was a drunk. She was fired, and Jane took over her job, living rent free. [22]

The Beginning of the End

Jane's downfall began in the summer of 1901. For many years she had rented a holiday home in Cataumet from the Davis family, who owned a hotel there. Jane had been lax in paying her rent, and although she was a favoured guest, the Davis' decided that it was time to call in Jane's debt of $500 (approx. $13,500 today). In June, Mattie Davis travelled to Cambridge to visit Jane at the Beedle's house and collect her back rent. Jane offered Mattie some mineral water, laced with morphine, and when Mattie became sick Jane gave her some more of the drug. Over the course of seven days, Mattie became sicker and sicker as Jane continued to poison her, even doing so under the watchful eye of a doctor until, on July 5th, Mattie fell into a coma and died. [23]

Jane accompanied Mattie's body back home and was there at the funeral. The family was grateful to the nurse for caring for Mattie, and a week later she moved into the Davis house to look after Mattie's widower, Alden, who was beside himself with grief at the loss of his wife.

Over the following weeks, Jane started no less than three fires in the Davis' house in an effort to kill the rest of the family, but each attempt was dealt with swiftly, much to Jane's disgust.

On July 26th, only three weeks after Mattie's death, Jane poisoned Genevieve Gordon, the Davis' youngest daughter. Jane told the family that Genevieve had committed suicide because she could not bear the grief of losing her mother. The death certificate stated that it was a heart attack.

Less than two weeks after the death of his daughter, Alden Davis also died at the hands of Jane Toppan, which the doctor put down to a cerebral hemorrhage.

Jane asked the oldest daughter of the Davis family, Minnie Gibbs, to write off the $500 debt she owed to the family. Minnie refused. [24] On August 12th, 1901, Jane murdered Minnie by way of morphine tablets. In a particularly twisted act, as Minnie lay dying Jane brought Minnie's ten-year-old son into her bed with her. There is no way of knowing whether any sexual assault took place on the boy. [25]

Having wiped out the entire Davis family, Jane returned to Lowell in late August. She had her sights set on marrying Oramel Brigham, her foster sister's widower. However, one person stood in her way – Oramel's sister, Edna Bannister, 77, so Jane did what she always did, and murdered her. She also poisoned Oramel himself, but only enough to make him sick so that she could prove her love for him by nursing him back to health. Nothing worked, and Oramel told Jane to leave, but not before Jane herself made a suicide attempt of her own.

Jane's Arrest

On August 31st, 1901, Captain Gibbs (Minnie Gibbs' father-in-law) ordered the bodies of the entire Davis family to be exhumed, to see whether his suspicions of their murders could be confirmed. By this time Jane had travelled to New Hampshire to stay with an old friend, Sarah Nichols, but had read about the exhumations in the newspaper.

On October 29th, 1901, Jane was arrested for the murder of Minnie Gibbs, and on December 6th, 1901, Jane was formally charged with four counts of murder – the entire Davis family.

Newspapers reported on March 31st, 1902, that Jane had undergone a psychiatric evaluation and had been classed as insane. She had admitted to the panel of experts that she had a sexual compulsion to kill, and confessed to 11 murders.

The Trial

The trial of Jane Toppan opened on June 23rd, 1902. The entire trial took less than eight hours, and the jury needed only 20 minutes to deliberate and deliver the verdict of Not Guilty by reason of insanity. She was sentenced to life at Taunton Insane Hospital, something she seemed delighted at. She believed that she would be freed in a matter of months because she would be able to convince the hospital that she was not, in fact, insane.

It later emerged that Jane had confessed to her defense lawyer, James Stuart Murphy, that she had committed more than 31 murders.

This confession was published in the New York Journal, including her admission that she had duped the panel into thinking she was insane, and that she felt very smug indeed at having outsmarted the experts. She also described the 'exquisite pleasure' killing had given her, and the lack of remorse she felt at the murders.

Jane laid the blame for the murders on the fiancé who had jilted her when she was in her teens, claiming *"If I had been a married woman, I probably would not have killed all of those people. I would have had my husband, my children and my home to take up my mind."*

Despite her belief that she would be freed, Jane Toppan spent the rest of her life at the asylum. Had she been freed, her killing spree would no doubt have continued – she is reported to have said that her only ambition in life was *"to have killed more people...helpless people....than any other man or woman who ever lived."*

Jane died on August 17th, 1938, at the age of 81. During the first two years in the asylum, her mental health was scrutinised, with many people asking why she was there as she appeared totally sane. There then followed a slow decline into insanity, with Jane often seen soothing other patients, crying out that they were dying, and trying to administer imaginary doses. Ironically, she became convinced that she herself was being poisoned and would stop eating, resulting in a dramatic weight loss. In a letter written to one of her doctors, she made reference to the 'poisonings':

"Taunton Lunatic Hospital, July 1, 1904.——"Doctor Stedman: I wish to inform you that I am alive, in spite of the deleterious food which has been served me. Many efforts have been made to poison me – of that I am very sure. I am thin and very hungry all the time. Every nerve is calling for food. Why can't I have help? I ate a pint of ice cream and four oranges Saturday and Sunday. (Signed) JANE TOPPAN
"NORAH KELLEY." [27]

In the end, Jane Toppan's deeds came back to haunt her.

www.ingramcontent.com/pod-product-compliance
Lightning Source LLC
Chambersburg PA
CBHW051800130726
47987CB00003B/1051